The
GENIUS
of MOSES

JOHN H. REDFIELD

The
GENIUS
of MOSES

How Moses Considered God

TATE PUBLISHING
AND ENTERPRISES, LLC

Published by Tate Publishing & Enterprises, LLC
127 E. Trade Center Terrace | Mustang, Oklahoma 73064 USA
1.888.361.9473 | www.tatepublishing.com

Tate Publishing is committed to excellence in the publishing industry. The company reflects the philosophy established by the founders, based on Psalm 68:11,
"The Lord gave the word and great was the company of those who published it."

Book design copyright © 2013 by Tate Publishing, LLC. All rights reserved.
Cover design by Rtor Maghuyop
Cover image depicts "Moses with the Ten Commandments on the Two Stone Tablets," a statue from the Martini Church in Braunschweig, Germany
Interior design by Jake Muelle

Published in the United States of America

ISBN: 978-1-62510-230-0
1. Religion / Biblical Biography / Old Testament
2. Rel006030
13.05.02

DEDICATION

TO

Temple Beth El, Bloomfield Hills, Michigan
My house shall be called
A house of prayer for all peoples. Isaiah (56:7-8)

FOR

Arlene, John and Pam, Jane and Richard,
Robert, Brian, Jessica, Alison, and Rebecca.

TABLE OF CONTENTS

Special Recognition

To entitle this section "Acknowledgments" would be so general as to make the list voluminous. It is more appropriate to recognize those without whose input *The Genius of Moses* would not exist, not even in the mind of the author.

For most of my formative years, I lived with my maternal grandfather, Israel Cohen, whose influence was huge. He taught me Hebrew, ethical living, and biblical scholarship and piqued my interest in the works of Shakespeare, all of which resonate throughout the following pages.

I would not have persisted without the forbearance of my devoted wife, Arlene, who gave up many hours of quality togetherness time. It was she who insisted the text contained too many commas. Her friends Sue, Rita, and Marilyn read it and deleted the surfeit of commas.

My good friend and an English professor, Bill Darby, using his red pencil, edited the manuscript extensively, scrupulously adhering to the intended meaning. He put back many of the commas that the girls had eliminated.

Professor Jason H. Ticton, music director of Temple Beth El, with the prompting of then Rabbi B. Benedict Glazier, selected me to become the cantorial soloist. This led to enduring friendships and learning experiences with Jason and Glazer's successor Rabbi Richard C. Hertz, culminating in my appointment as cantor thirty-five years later. The significance of these years at Temple Beth El is revealed in every page that follows.

Another good friend, Rabbi Sherwin Wine, was an associate rabbi at Temple Beth El, before embarking on his career as an advocate of Humanistic Judaism, stimulated my interest in existentialism. When I broached my discovery that Moses' thinking expressed components of existentialism, he encouraged me to write this book. He also was instrumental in bringing Rabbi Abraham Joshua Heschel to lecture at Temple Beth El.

During this lecture, Heschel addressed the question, "Who speaks for God?" His answer that the prophets spoke for God became the touchstone of my thinking from that time forward. In a project to become acquainted with his thinking and writing, I became intrigued by his creation of such pithy expressions as, "radical amazement," "moral grandeur," and "spiritual audacity." These phrases, and many more from his lips and pen resonate from cover to cover

Another rabbi of Temple Beth El was Rabbi Daniel Polish; without his encouragement, I would not have proceeded beyond the first few chapters. In our many luncheon conversations, he played the devil's advocate, challenging my assertions to fine tune my thinking. He also suggested a bibliography that proved to be invaluable.

Yet another intimate friend and rabbi, Dannel Schwartz, indulged me by frequent conversations in Hebrew, providing moments of happy memories for me and, I hope for him as well. He gave me his only copy of the *Essays* of Henry Slonimsky, his highly esteemed professor at the Hebrew Union College. It will always be one of the most cherished books in my library. He also acquainted me with the expression, "Moses learned that he could take the Israelites out of Egypt, but he couldn't take Egypt out of the Israelites.

Of extreme importance is to express my gratitude to all of the other rabbis of Beth El who encouraged my efforts during the forty years of my tenure. All of them supported my thesis of *The Genius of Moses* and encouraged me to write this book.

Subsequent to its completion, my present rabbi, Daniel B Syme, did the important favor of validating the biblical references and making numerous suggestions. Most recently, my appreciation of Dr. Richard Tate's confidence in my manuscript that led to its publication.

THE ESSENCE OF TORAH[1]

There was a man who lived in the mountains. He knew nothing about those who lived in the city. He sowed wheat and ate the kernels raw.

One day, he entered the city. They brought him good bread. He said, "What is this for?" They said, "Bread to eat!" He ate, and it tasted very good. He said, "What is it made of?" They said, "Wheat."

Later, they brought him cakes kneaded in oil. He tasted them and said, "What are they made of?" They said, "Wheat."

Finally, they brought him royal pastry made with honey and oil. "And what are these made of?" They said, "Wheat." He said, "I am the master of all of these, for I eat the essence of all of these: wheat!"

Because of that view, he knew nothing of the delights of the world; they were lost to him. So it is with one who grasps the principle and does not know all the delectable delights deriving, diverging from that principle.

THE GRAND NARRATIVE

A MASTER STORY THAT UNDERLIES AND INFORMS INNUMERABLE CONCRETE TELLINGS AND RETELLINGS[1]

The Grand Narrative began as a journey—a journey from Egypt to Canaan, from slavery to freedom, from idolatry to the worship of an invisible God. It is related in the biblical books of Exodus through Deuteronomy and was told and retold for generations and then written down circa 600 BCE. From that point on, it has been read and reread every year in the synagogue and serves as the theme of the Passover seder.

The words remain the same, but their meaning changes. In Buber's words: "Upon each reading, we face the book with a new attitude as something new."[2]

The parable of the wheat farmer adds clarity to Buber's words. Wheat is nutritious in its natural state but is dry and unpalatable. The wheat farmer was complacent and did not seek to enjoy his produce on a higher level, baked and enriched with oil and honey. So it is with the words of Torah—they virtually cry out for the enrichment of contemporary interpretation.

A message of epic proportion, the words reflect the history and customs of the ancient Middle East. During the retelling, much detail was lost, historical gaps occurred, and many events became chronologically misplaced.

Hence, the need suggested by the wheat farmer, *midrash*, meaning "to seek out or inquire." In this endeavor, rabbis, scholars, and students throughout the ages have refined the words of Torah, in this metaphor symbolized by wheat, and baked them into royal cakes.

History needs to be rewritten—not because of the accumulation of new "facts," but because of new ways of seeing the past.

The tradition of *midrashim* (plural of *midrash)* encourages the interpretive study of the Bible. What stimulates us to seek a certain higher level of understanding? Most likely, it's a particular clue. Clues appear singularly, as Virginia Woolf experienced, "like a match struck unexpectedly in the dark." Once we discover a significant clue, we search for others, and fortunately in the Grand Narrative, they appear in abundance.

It's like a doctor making a diagnosis or a detective solving a case. Once they discover a relevant clue, that clue points the way to a proliferation of others. *Alone Atop the Mountain* by Rabbi Samuel Sandmel provided such a clue. The key word in the title is *Alone.* Here is a clue I felt compelled investigation. It is generally understood that God spoke only to Moses. But the apparent fact that Moses was alone with God when he heard His words had escaped me. That's how it was when I chanced upon the novel

The Torah is replete with phrases such as "and the Lord spoke to Moses saying," but the unique one-on-one relationship was intriguing. If only we could get into Moses' head and discover his perception of the Grand Narrative. Once this objective was defined further, clues became readily apparent.

In pursuing this line of thought, we get valuable insight from Genesis, which prepares us for the ensuing God-Moses relationship. In Genesis, we see the gradual disappearance of God who, at the outset, was in complete control. God created the heavens, the earth, and all they contain, culminating in the creation of humankind among whom he walked.

From that point on, God's control diminished. Humans sinned, and he punished them, and then God gradually vanished from the scene. In some remote way, God spoke to Abraham who was compliant and did his bidding. Along came Rebecca who, with the concurrence of God, successfully deceived Isaac to convey the birthright to Jacob. Later, God communicated with Jacob in dreams.

Finally, in the Joseph saga, God disappeared altogether. Joseph was reduced to reporting to Pharaoh the words that came to him from God. We are left wondering how God revealed himself to Joseph.

Despite the four-hundred-year gap between Joseph's death and Moses' birth, not much changed. God had not reappeared upon the scene. Like Joseph, only

Moses was addressed by God: "It was only Moses who heard the words, and he reported them to the people."[3]

The bewildering question is where did the words come from? In what way did the invisible God speak to Moses? How did the words get from God's mouth to Moses' ear? Unfortunately, just getting into his head doesn't give us the complete answer. It does suggest three possibilities:

- ☐ Revelation: Moses experienced an overwhelming disclosure of the invisible God.
- ☐ Inspiration: The intuitive awareness of God's will emanating from his immanent presence.
- ☐ Cognition: Moses thought the concept of an invisible God would establish the source of his authority to accomplish the rescue of the Israelites.

The vagueness of these terms opens the door to preference based on one's own perceptions; any one of the above does not exclude the others. Consider that the discussion that follows is consistent with any of one or a combination of the above. Previously held convictions within the scope of these possibilities have credibility.

Of greater relevance is the insight to be gained by getting into Moses' head in order to understand his thinking. The product of Moses' genius was his creativity, the process by which he saw things in novel ways—in the words of William James, "The faculty of perceiving in unhabitual ways."[4]

However, such an effort is greater than an intellectual experience; by getting into his head, we virtually become Moses. Through his eyes, we experience the time and places of his youth, the sources of his roots, and the molding of them. We adopt his values and share his desires. We experience his anxieties, rejoice in his achievements, feel his anger, and merge with the maturing grace of his later years. To do all these things, we have to re-examine the Grand Narrative as seen by Moses.

Imagine being part of Moses' thought process, which discerned: "We do not see things as they are; we see things as we are."[5] All perceptions exist in the mind—reality is in the eye of the beholder.

Exploring the Grand Narrative, we find this idea repeated again and again. It became Moses' way of making the presence of the invisible God known to the Israelites. Moses adopted a process by which experiences would be conditioned to become perceptions.

An example from Exodus 17: In the wilderness, the people were dying of thirst. Moses knew the territory; he had learned from past experience where the potable water was, but in their presence, he called to God for help. When he struck a rock and water issued forth, he persuaded the people it was God's intervention.

Rabbi Abraham Joshua Heschel, who had the gift of encapsulating significant meaning in a terse phrase, coined the expression *radical amazement* to describe the perception of a natural occurrence as an apparent miracle. For the people, what Moses conditioned them to perceive would become reality—that God had provided the water.

The idea that perception is the reality became the cornerstone of Moses' leadership. Without this concept, it is unlikely the Exodus would have become the Grand Narrative.

Moses encouraged the idea of becoming. The Israelites, nurtured in an environment of subservience in Egypt, lacked the incentive to mature and recreate their own lives. He prodded them to observe God's laws and commandments, taught them ethical living, and expanded the idea of holiness to convey the presence of the Invisible. In doing so, he exemplified the elevation of individual dignity for himself and others.

Moses imposed the responsibility of freedom of choice. The people were to be accountable for their own decisions and actions to define themselves. In his final words, he rued the possibility that, once in the Promised Land, some would seek immediate gratification in preference to the common good. He fully understood the negative potential of free choice—the ambiguity of human freedom might lead to irresponsible choices. This was the choice Moses made.

Reading further in this book, this is what you will find:

- ❑ Initially, my discovery of the magnificent mind of Moses and how he thought like an existentialist.
- ❑ The chapters two and three provide a brief introduction to existentialism—all that you need to know to get inside Moses' head to see how he thought.

❏ An overview of the book of Genesis to observe how the perception of God changed and carried forward into Exodus.

❏ With the above as preparation, we can begin the journey with Moses from Egypt to the Promised Land and witness the development he effected of feeling the presence of the invisible God.

❏ The final chapter presents my own perceptions from a study of the Grand Narrative.

Open my eyes, that I may perceive the wonders of Your Torah.

—Psalm (119:18)

A MATCH STRUCK
IN THE DARK

Inspirations are so rare that it's one of life's treasures to be able to share them. So before discussing Moses, whose life was replete with them, I believe it will be helpful to share my first awareness of the prodigious genius of Moses' mind—how he thought "in an unhabitual way."

To Virginia Woolf, revelations seldom came. Instead, "there were little daily miracles, illuminations, matches struck unexpectedly in the dark."[1] In retrospect, her metaphor epitomizes my experience upon the realization that existential thought was embodied in the words of Moses. Sharing my experience is intended to kindle a match for others to better see and understand his mind.

It is the custom in the synagogue to read a designated portion of the Torah each week. When a Jewish boy or girl reaches the age of thirteen to become *bar mitzvah*, they must read in Hebrew the Torah portion of the week and translate it into English.

My "little miracle" happened when, as the cantor of Temple Beth El, Detroit, I was assisting a *bar mitzvah* student whom we shall call David. His Torah portion was from Exodus 3, known in Hebrew as *Shemot* (names) in which God spoke to Moses from a burning thorn bush. After fluently reading the Hebrew, he proceeded to translate until he came to the Hebrew words *EHYEH ASHER EHYEH,* for which he offered the English equivalent that he had been taught, "I am what I am."

At that point, he stopped, turned to me, and asked the meaning of that seemingly arcane phrase. Little did he realize he was not alone; scholars throughout history have found it puzzling.

I, too, had found the expression enigmatic and, for the moment, was without a suitable explanation. To buy time, I suggested he finish his translation and we would discuss it later. As he went on, for all I knew he might have been translating "The Rubaiyat" of Omar Khayyam, because related thoughts were rushing through my mind.

My first thought was of Rabbi Sherwin Wine who was brilliant at explaining abstract concepts to young people. He would not have had to buy time as I did. The thought of Sherwin, who had inspired my interest in existentialism, ignited the idea that in today's parlance I am what I am has an existential meaning.

That was the easy part. Now, how was I to explain it to David?

In his book *Basic Judaism,*[2] Milton Steinberg discussed attributes of God, offering the reader a variety of choices—all consistent with Jewish thought, but none mandatory.

Steinberg implied that the idea of God is so vast and multifaceted that no one can grasp its totality, leaving the option of individual experience as the criterion.

He noted it is written in Proverbs 3:6, "In all your ways know Him." Nowhere is it written, in all *God's* ways know him. And that's for a compelling reason, according to Jewish tradition, we cannot know God completely.[3]

The meaning we can grasp of God is related to our ways, our perceptions derived from personal experience. Whatever the totality of an individual's perceptions at any given time is his or her reality. Hence, the God we know is only a glimmer of a greater reality in the same way that a beam of light only implies the glory of the sun.

> *Such knowledge is too wonderful for me; Too high, I cannot attain unto it . . .*
>
> *How weighty also are the thoughts of Thee unto me, O God!*
>
> *How great is the sum of them! If I would count them, they are more in number than the grains of sand.*
>
> Psalm 139:17-18

Rabbi Abraham Joshua Heschel expressed it even more cogently: "A person's perception depends upon his experience, upon his assumptions, categories of thinking, degree of sensitivity, environment and cultural atmosphere. A person will notice what he is conditioned to see."[4]

When David finished his translation, he again turned to me, this time in search for the answer to his question. Since he played the clarinet in his middle school band, I expected he would be able to relate to a tangential explanation related to his musical experience.

I began by asking him what piece he played in the band he liked the most. It was "Stars and Stripes Forever." With further prompting, I hoped he would get the message. I explained that each band member learns and practices his assigned part, which later becomes merged with all the other parts to create the unified sound of the piece of music.

If one focuses on individual instrumental parts, to each musician the piece is a unique experience. Listening to Sousa's March, band members recall learning and playing particular parts. They would even assume ownership and refer to them as "their parts." If you've ever played or sung in an ensemble, you'll know how this sense of ownership occurs.

In its entirety, the sound that the audience hears is decidedly different than what the individual musicians hear. Even the conductor does not hear the same thing; his attention is focused mostly on the balance of sound.

Further, in the audience, each listener relates hearing a piece to prior listenings. To each of them, hearing David's band play was a unique experience. Personally, every time I hear that Sousa piece, I recall marching to it during basic training at Camp Crowder, Missouri, usually at six o'clock in the morning. What is heard is conditioned by the sum total of a listener's experiences.

David concluded that upon hearing the piece performed he would always be listening to the clarinets.

The point is we see things as we are conditioned to see them. In David's way, he experienced the Sousa march from a clarinet player's perspective; I, from a soldier's point of view. To each of us, the reality of Sousa's march would always be unique.

God certainly wasn't talking about band music. Like music that can be heard but not seen, the presence of God can be felt, but not seen. God knew that individuals contemplating his reality would be limited by their own unique perceptions based on prior experience.

Hence, "I am what I am" means I am what you already know from past experience. Actually, God wasn't talking only to Moses, he was speaking through Moses to the Israelites and all humankind at that time and thereafter.

I suggested that David try to imagine how difficult it would be for someone who had been a slave in Egypt to be confronted with the idea of an invisible God. Their culture reflected the worship of Egyptian deities like the sun, the moon, birds, and beasts—deities who were worshipped on mountaintops and whose likenesses were portrayed in images.

In stark contrast, here was a God who could only be seen in the mind's eye. His presence had to be experienced—felt—in order to be perceived. For Moses, the challenge of communicating such a radical theology would be a challenge to his remarkable ingenuity.

When asked if he could think of a way the Israelites might have experienced God, David had an answer from the Passover service. "How about God dividing the Red Sea so the Israelites could cross on dry land, and the waters closed drowning the Egyptians? Wasn't that an experience of God?" David was right on.

Moses would come to understand that such experiences could be seen as apparent miracles in the eyes of the beholders caused by an invisible God whose enveloping presence could be felt but not reasoned. Such a transformative experience Heschel called "radical amazement."[5]

To further reinforce this idea, I asked David if he remembered the story in Genesis of Jacob's dream of a ladder on which angels were going down and up between heaven and earth. The Lord stood beside Jacob and spoke to him. At that time, I could only paraphrase the story, but here are the exact words:

> Jacob awoke from his sleep and said, "Surely the Lord is present in this place, and I did not know it!" Shaken he said, "How awesome is this place! This is no other than the abode of God, and that is the Gateway to heaven."
>
> Genesis 28:16

"David, does it not seem to you that Jacob experienced a startling revelation. One in which when he awoke from the dream he was *shaken?* Can you see how because of this experience his idea of God would never be the same again?"

"I think I get it," he said. "When I was little, I used to think of God as an old man with a long white beard. But my second grade teacher taught us that God was not a man at all, he couldn't even be seen. She said, 'God was more like the wind. Something you could feel around you—that made things happen—but couldn't be seen.' She also read us a poem about the wind."

The poem David had in mind was "Who Has Seen the Wind" by Christina Rossetti.

> Who has seen the wind? Neither you nor I,
> But when the trees bow down their heads,
> The wind is passing by.

He caught on so quickly that I dared to complicate the issue. "The Hebrew phrase "*ehyeh asher ehyeh*," often translated as if in the present tense "I am what I am," is actually in the Hebrew future tense and should be rendered as "I will be what I will be."

I explained, "This makes even more sense, because it anticipates that as the Israelites continued to experience God's concern for them, their concepts of God would change. So it is with us. As we grow, so does our understanding of God. Similarly, in services, we reread the Torah every year. The words are the same, but we have changed—to us, their meaning has been modified."

Fortunately, I didn't lose David. He responded appropriately. "I'm a little different than I was yesterday and more different than I was the day before." Many thanks to David's Sunday school teacher who had the foresight to disabuse him of the image of God with a white beard.

In summing up, I told David, "At your *bar mitzva*, the cantorial I will sing after you have read from the Torah will be from Proverbs 3, the same chapter in which we discovered the words "in all your ways, know Him." Hopefully, it will remind you of this conversation."

However, what I didn't tell David was that a subtle inference can be drawn from the scene at the bush. Considering those three enigmatic words in their biblical context, another match became struck in the dark.

> Moses said to God, "When I come to the Israelites and say to them, 'The God of your fathers has sent me to you, and they ask me,
>
> "What is His name? what shall I say to them?" And God said to Moses, "EHYEH-ASHER-EHYEY [I will be what I will be]." He continued, "Thus shall you say to the Israelites, "EHYEH sent me to you.'"
>
> Exodus 3:13–14

What is stunningly amazing is that the interchange of expression continued, and Moses never questioned God as to the meaning of his somewhat ambiguous name. He intuitively had grasped the message that reality is in the eye of the beholder; God was essentially saying, "You and all others will know me from what you experience, and as the total of your experience increases, so will your knowledge of me expand." Moses perceived this in an unhabitual way as meaning, "in all your ways, know Him."

The awesomeness of God's presence did not make Moses reluctant to question Him; that didn't seem to deter him later in the dialogue. Moses questioned other things, such as why God had chosen him to plead His case before Pharaoh. So one can be assured he understood the meaning of the words *EHYEH ASHER EHYEY*. In his mind, he sensed that God's name was the message.

I couldn't wait to relate the experience to Rabbi Sherwin Wine and ask him if he agreed with my reasoning, which led to an interpretation of the enigmatic *EHYEY-ASHER-EHYEY*. When I did, his comment was, "Absolutely! I don't know why I never picked up on that."

Moses readily perceived the idea that the perception of reality is implicit in *ehyey asher ehyey*. It was a unique thought process that would characterize his thinking throughout the Exodus and would eventually become a basic tenet of existentialism; hence, knowledge of the principles of existentialism will help us get into Moses' head and better understand how he thought in what for him was an unhabitual way. The next two chapters will take care of that.

> Happy is the man who finds wisdom,
> The man who attains understanding.
>
> Proverbs 3:13

WHERE IS SINAI TODAY?

I n 1973 my wife, Arlene, and I took our first trip to Israel, during which my burning desire was to visit Mount Sinai, the scene of many of the stories we study in the Torah. I knew the exact location was uncertain, but I encountered a guide who told me he knew where to take me.

As expected, he was ready and waiting as I exited the International Hotel in Jerusalem. Since our objective was in the Sinai Peninsula, my first criterion for a guide that day was someone with a fairly new, air-conditioned car. In Israel, a car with 90,000 or fewer miles on the odometer is considered new.

Above all, I wanted to be sure of completing the trip without mishap and in reasonable comfort despite the intense desert heat. Fortunately, my second criterion was also met—his car was indeed air-conditioned.

When we introduced ourselves the day before, I explained that our itinerary was to visit Mount Sinai. Shalom, the guide, assured me it was no problem, although he kindly suggested there might be places of more general interest where there was a greater comfort level. Not a chance! For years, I had yearned to visit that mountain—it was now or probably never.

As we discussed our itinerary, neither of us so much as alluded to the fact that the exact location we sought is not known. Shalom again explained that he knew exactly where to take me and how lucky I was to have one of the most well informed guides in Israel as well and the benefit of a first class vehicle—actually his brother's. Israeli guides are not known for their modesty and, more often than not, are using someone else's car.

The drive south of Jerusalem through the hills of Galilee took us through some of Israel's loveliest scenery and towns and villages with mixed farming in the valleys and olive trees on the rocky slopes.

Beyond Hebron, the scenery changed dramatically. It was only a brief time before we left cultivated land and reached inhospitable desert. No more greenery and trees, only scrub brush, an occasional motley tree, and a few wild goats to break the monotony of desert travel.

However, the trip was not without interest. Shalom had been a pilot in the Yom Kippur war and participated in several sorties into Arab countries. Suffice it to say, he liked to tell war stories and had no reluctance to express his political opinions.

As we drove on, the heat and monotony did not mitigate my excitement. For many years, I had longed to visit the area where my forefathers lived when they came forth out of Egypt. The heat and desolation only increased my empathy for their constant complaining and my admiration for Moses' stalwart dedication not to let them turn back. It is evident these two emotions have remained ingrained in the character of the Jewish people from that time to this.

Surrounded by desert, my mind began to wander, pondering what it must have been like for the Israelites who lived in these surroundings for forty years. Just looking at that ugly desert from an air-conditioned car, one could understand the yearning of many to return to Egypt, even if it meant resuming the yoke of slavery.

As I reflected on our biblical forebears, Shalom took my silence as a signal to do what he did best—teach. (In Hebrew, a guide is known as a *moray derech*, a teacher of the way.) Constrained not to permit a protracted silence, he proceeded to prattle on about our geographical objective.

"A familiar name for Sinai is *Jebel Musa* (Arabic for 'the mountain of Moses').Perched on a rocky slope, we will soon see Saint Catherine's Monastery. It was built there by Greek Orthodox monks some fifteen hundred years ago. They allege it stands on the actual site where Moses felt God's presence in the burning bush.

"The monks liked the place because they thought they would be close to God and, also, not incidentally, near water. They were persuasive enough to solicit funds for its expansion over the years."

He continued in this vein with the positive assurance of an Israeli, but I would hope he assumed from our earlier conversation that I knew better. Actually, scholars believe that Jebel Musa lies too far south to be consistent with the route God gave Moses (Exodus 14:1). More likely, the site was Jebel Halal, but no matter.

The rabbis clearly did not want the precise site of either Sinai or Horeb known, lest the Jews might do as the monks and make the site of God's revelation a focus of worship. The message of Torah is clear: God would not reside in some high place or in a sanctuary, as earlier people imagined, but among them.

"*I will abide among the Israelites, and I will be their God. And they shall know that I the Lord am their God who brought them out of the land of Egypt that I might dwell among them*" Exodus (29:45–46).

I had either dozed or become inattentive when I was recalled to reality by his excitement when he virtually shouted, "Look straight ahead, there's your mountain." Despite the heat, I felt a sudden chill. There we were in the plains where the Israelites encamped while Moses was out of their sight for forty days atop the mountain. In the distance, the rugged beauty of the granite mountains rose abruptly from the barren plain.

At my request, Shalom stopped the car to let me out. I wanted to stand where they stood and walk in their footsteps. Suddenly, time seemed to rush back three thousand years. Crowds appeared to be encamped at the base of that mountain in the barren wilderness. In Arab dress, they were impatiently milling about, cursing in a strange tongue, and directing their wrath toward the mountain. Many had encircled a strange object, a crude Egyptian-like sculpture, which appeared to hold a strange fascination for them. They were chanting and moving about in rhythm, much like a dance, stomping their feet similar to an African tribal ritual—a mysterious, disturbing, ominous sight of a crowd out of control. Others were attempting to dissuade them from their idolatry, but to no avail.

I was having the beginning of a stream of consciousness experience—a dramatization of the function of the mind, one thought triggering another. The following is my best recollection of the memories that were enkindled by the emotional experience.

+≡≡≡+

I envisioned the napery, starched and very white, was in vivid contrast to the dog-eared, food and wine stained *haggadot* (plural for order of service for the Passover seder ritual). The wine sparkled in the crystal carafe from which each of us poured a glass. My grandfather, the consummate patriarch, was presiding over our family seder.

He departed from the familiar text to comment on the intentional omission of Moses' name. The name of Moses does not appear in the traditional *haggada* because it was thought that lionizing Moses would detract from the significance of God. For a similar reason, the obscurity of the location of Sinai prevents worship of the mount instead of the messages that were received there.

Grandfather proceeded to express his personal bias for not reading the section about the plagues because he thought they were contrived. The climax of the preprandial portion was *dayenu* (Hebrew for, *it would have been sufficient*) recited in unison and then sung—a fitting response to the many wonders God had performed for the Israelites as they came forth from the land of Egypt, any one of which would have been more than sufficient, *dayenu*.

When the table was cleared, we proceeded with the service but with subdued enthusiasm. Even the singing of *Adir Hu* and *Ha Gadyo* suffered in spirit from the surfeit of food and wine. But when at the conclusion, we all exclaimed *l'shanah haba'ah b'rushalayim* (next year in Jerusalem); there was a strong sense of conviction.

In my next elusion , I was standing alone at the western wall in Jerusalem when time became compacted as my life passed before me, much like Pablo anticipating his imminent execution in Sartre's *The Wall*.

I couldn't decide if my tears were born of joy or sadness—joy to be there, or sadness for my grandfather who throughout his life declared at the seder, "Next year in Jerusalem," and in his daily prayers, "Jerusalem—rebuild it soon in our days." If only he had lived to personally experience such joy.

Not just my grandfather but thousands of grandfathers who, like Moses, longed for, imagined, but never reached the Promised Land. Why me and not them? But most of all, Moses who led the Israelites from slavery in Egypt through forty years of adversity in the desert, only to be denied experiencing his ultimate goal.

I remembered returning home from Sunday school and affirming to my mother that I knew what God looked like. Here was God's picture on the cover of my new Sunday school book—a figure of monumental proportion, flowing beard and horns protruding from his forehead, wearing a robe, and seated on a bench? She was dismayed by the statement and my inability to accept the idea that God was invisible.

She patiently explained that the figure on the book cover was that of Moses, not God. She told me that God is invisible, cannot be seen, drawn, or painted. Imagine trying to convey that abstraction to an eight-year-old. Unfortunately, she didn't know the poem "Who is Like the Wind."

Years later, I encountered the figure replicated on the book cover. It was Michelangelo's inspired sculpture of Moses. It is placed in a small church in Rome, St. Pietro in Vincolo, which would be a minor tourist attraction were it not for the statue of Moses posed seated on a boulder, presumably in his first battle with the Amalekites.

Michelangelo derived his image of Moses from his reading of the Vulgate. Despite the disfiguring protuberances on the forehead suggested by a mistranslation in his biblical reference, the statue has become the quintessential image of Moses. In Buber's words, "The man, flaming with the urgent truth of his mission."[1]

Sigmund Freud had a strong affinity for this figure of Moses. He interpreted the protuberances as Michelangelo's symbolism of the inner rage expressed in the Torah as Moses' anger. Freud made at least three trips to Rome to sit in awe at the foot of this statue.

In his words, "… the giant frame with its tremendous physical power becomes only a concrete expression of the highest mental achievement that is possible in a man, that of struggling successfully against an inward passion for the sake of a cause to which he has devoted himself."[2] It prompted this recollection: "He saw an Egyptian beating a Hebrew slave, one of his kinsmen. He turned this way and that and, seeing no one about, he struck down the Egyptian and hid him in the sand (Exodus 2:12).

Whether for a peremptory or a contemplated reason Moses killed the Egyptian, it was an existential decision after which nothing would ever be the same. Would I have been standing there in the hot sand had Moses not been moved by the plight of his people and, instead, opted to remain in the comfort and security of the courts of Pharaoh?

A brief glance at the mountain triggered a memory of Rabbi Leo M. Franklin, my admired teacher and a good friend of the family, reciting the words of Psalm 121:

> *I turn my eyes to the mountains, From where will my help come? My help comes from the Lord, Maker of heaven and earth.*

The idea that deities resided on mountain tops was an ancient near-east concept that inspired the poetry of the psalmist.

Jebel Musa had not changed since the Exodus, but I knew it could not have been Sinai. The mountain bore no resemblance to the picture in my Sunday school book; it would have been impossible for Moses to descend its precipitous rock cliffs holding the stone tablets before him even if he were of the muscular majestic proportions portrayed by Michelangelo.

It is now meaningful to pause and reflect on what I had imagined. As I stood where the Israelites seemingly encamped, the base of Jebel Musa became the site of their encounter with the golden calf. I was transported through time and space to a family seder in which the Exodus story is briefly related, to my first experience at the wall, to a conversation with my mother, and, finally, to Michelangelo's famous "Moses." The series of reflections had an understandable concatenation.

Of course, I recalled my conversation with David and the various perceptions of "Stars and Stripes Forever," resulting from the unique experiences of musicians and listeners. The existential musical example came from Sartre who pondered the question, "Where is Beethoven's 'Seventh Symphony' today?"[3] His question also inspired my title of this chapter "Where Is Sinai Today?"

Sartre's question poses several rhetorical questions. Was it interred with Beethoven's bones? Is it the original score written in the composer's own hand? Is it in the interpretations of various conductors? Or is it in the minds of everyone who has ever heard it played? One need only consider the reference of David referring to "my clarinet part" to see these issues.

Sartre answers his own question, as one would expect, in a very personal way. "What is the 'Seventh Symphony' itself? Obviously it is a thing that is something that is before me, that endures, which lasts." Note the personal relation "before me;" Sartre was an existentialist.

I prefer the perception of music articulated by Rabbi Irwin Groner: "Music is not simply the creative genius of the writer or of the performer, as important and indispensable as they are. We should recognize a spirit that reposes in the listeners that evokes this creative achievement and that contributes to the creative process."[4]

Thus, the answer to our question "Where is Sinai today?" follows the same line of reasoning as the musical analogies. The following chapter will be devoted to a discussion of several simple existential concepts, which, in conjunction with resolving the questions about Sinai and Beethoven, will provide the necessary background to grasp the existential ideas found in Moses' unhabitual thinking.

WHERE SINAI IS TODAY

My stream of consciousness in the previous chapter could have been more aptly termed an existential experience, because the nuclei of the memories were my previously held perceptions—a concept fundamental to existentialism. It's the same existential process that reveals where Beethoven's symphony and Sinai are. If the process is not now clear, the present chapter will add clarity, and several other important existential incites will be introduced.

Sartre cleverly resolved the question regarding the presence of things in the concluding pages of his novel *Nausea*. "If you broke the record, or tore up the score, the song would still be there." To Sartre, an existentialist, reality is in the perception of the beholder.

Jebal Musa was only one of thirteen possible sites of Sinai identified by scholars. If they were all proved erroneous, would the meaning of the Ten Commandments change? If the location of the mountain has changed, its subjective value remains steadfast. Reality is in the perception of the beholder.

Similarly, our understanding of the Exodus will be expanded if we see it, as Moses did, through an existential prism. However, we will need a few more fundamental existential ideas and related vocabulary.

To introduce this subject, let me tell you about my friend Josh (not his real name). His parents inhabited a comfortable, upper-middle class home reflecting standard materialistic values—a grand piano infrequently played and books seldom or never read. They socialized with a country club set, traveled extensively, and lived what they believed was the good life. To them, communal concerns were of minor importance.

As expected, Josh initially fit the pattern—winter and summer homes and two country clubs. However, his life assumed a change.

When he moved to a small town in the suburbs, he became a volunteer fireman and served in a hospital emergency room. Josh felt a commitment to community he did not learn at home. He imagined what his life should be, and he created it.

He responded to my question as to why he broke the pattern by saying, "I have always had a good life and wanted to give something back." And that was when he no longer owned a second home or belonged to a private country club. Josh saw his glass as half-full, not half-empty. In Sartre's terms, he chose to define his authentic self.

You may be wondering, "What does this have to do with existentialism?" Actually, there are three basic existential ideas embedded in Josh's story—ideas also rooted in the Exodus narrative. Josh became aware of what his life should be and having made his choice proceeded to make a significant difference in his lifestyle.

Jean Paul Sartre's name usually comes to mind when we think about the leading ideas of existentialism. He was not the first such thinker, but he—more than anyone else—put it all together in his novels, plays, and philosophic discourses.

When asked the meaning of existentialism, Sartre offered a three word core answer: "Existence precedes essence."[1] Sartre explained, "First of all man exists, turns up, appears on the scene, and, only afterwards, defines himself. At the beginning he is nothing. Only afterwards will he be something, and he, himself, will have determined what he will be."[2] It is clearly apparent that Josh defined himself—created his essence—what Sartre called his authentic self.

This is the first principle of existentialism. "Man is nothing else but what he makes of himself. It is also what is called subjectivity—man is conscious of imagining himself as being in the future."[3]

Defining one's authentic self is a matter of free will—the act of choosing what one wants to become. Freedom comes as close to constituting the essence of man as existence makes possible. The ultimate and final freedom that cannot be taken away is the freedom to say, "No." Josh said no to conspicuous consumption.

One step further is the matter of reality. From Sartre, again: "By existentialism we mean a doctrine which makes human life possible and, in addition, declares that every truth and every action implies a human setting. It can be defined easily—that existence precedes essence, or, if you prefer, that subjectivity must be the starting point."[4] To the existentialist, reality is unique to each individual; it is the cumulative result of all one's experiences at a given time.

Josh discovered his subjective starting point—his essence minimized the importance of the out-of-tune grand piano and books with pristine jackets. This can be neatly expressed existentially as "reality is in the eye of the beholder."

We now have defined three essential components of existentialism:

- ❑ To the individual, existence precedes essence.
- ❑ The individual is challenged by freedom of choice to define himself or herself.
- ❑ Reality is a perception of the individual.

The core statement "existence precedes essence" only obtains in the case of humans. For everything else, for all things, "essence precedes existence." Briefly discussing the latter will cast light on the former.

My daughter is an interior designer. When a client is thinking about a particular table for which none can be found in catalogs, Jane sketches what she envisions the client has in mind. If a sketch piques the client's interest, it becomes the essence of that table. Once the table materializes, it is no longer an essence—it exists.

If we are driving around the block looking for a place to park, we have in mind the essence of a parking space. If we get lucky and find one—voila, it exists. The distinction is clear. Only humans can define their own reality with subjectivity as the starting point.

Existential thought did not begin with Sartre although he is often credited with even more than his substantial contribution. The term actually is attributed to Søren Kierkegaard who observed, "My own existence is not at all a matter of speculation to me, but a reality in which I am personally and passionately involved."[5]

Like most seminal ideas, existentialism was an evolution before it had a name. From Walter Kaufman: "Existentialism is a timeless sensibility that can be discerned here and there in the past."[6] To better grasp his view, let's take a field trip to see how it percolated through several great minds of history.

We'll journey back in time about three thousand years and visit Moses at the tent of meeting on the hot desert sand. Moses was dealing with a rabble of humanity—an unruly mob recently freed from Pharaoh's yolk. His objective was to help them become witness to an unseen God.

Knowing that every perception is uniquely conditioned by a lifetime of experience, Moses ingeniously focused their perceptions on the awareness of God—a sense of an invisible God who cared about them, rescued them from slavery, and offered them the choice to be his people—in essence, to choose God. Obviously, Moses believed in freedom of choice.

To our question as to the nature of reality Moses might have replied, as was later expressed in a Talmudic Proverb, "We do not see things as they are. We see things as we are," Moses chose to focus the vision of the Israelites on certain events as acts of God, or quasi-miracles.

When I asked David if he could think of a way the Israelites might have experienced God, he spoke of the parting of the sea. We will discuss in a later chapter how Moses' familiarity with the territory anticipated the happening as a natural occurrence. Let's call the process that Moses employed "conditioned perception." He ingeniously conditioned them to see things as he wanted them to see.

Moses might have told us about his observation that how readily the sense of smell triggers memories of experiences. Think about your own memories, what the familiar aromas of a certain perfume and baking bread recall. "We do not see things as they are. We see things as we are." Things are intimately associated with our experiences.

As we journey forward in time, we encounter Socrates. He hit the nail on the head with his advice to students, "Know thyself." He taught there is no real philosophy until the mind turns around and examines itself.

Later his student, Plato, offered amazing existential insight in his allegory of the cave.[7] "And now I said, let me show you in a figure how far out our nature is enlightened or unenlightened. Behold! Human beings living in an underground den which has a mouth open towards the light."

Chained to a bench with their heads immobile, Plato's characters faced the wall opposite the opening, from which they could see only shadows of the creatures outside as they passed before the opening. To them, all beings and objects outside the cave were simply flat figures in shades of gray. This, then, was their perception of reality beyond the cave. "To them the world outside would be nothing but the shadows of images."

Roger Bacon made a convincing case for subjective experience. "A man may know that fire burns and then reason that contact with fire will hurt, but unless he places his hand in a fire the lesson will not be fully understood."[8]

William Barrett presents a comprehensive overview of existentialism in *Irrational Man*.[9] He expanded Bacon's distinction between learning from pure reason and the lessons of experience. Barrett's thesis is that traditional philosophy deals with reason to define reality, whereas existential thought relies on subjective experience. Does that not sound more like psychology than philosophy? Existentialism needs to be considered as an amalgamation of the two.

Another philosopher, Blaise Pascal understood man to be a creature of such contradictions and ambivalences that pure logic can never grasp. Hence, his favorite outcry "Not the God of the philosophers, but the God of Abraham, Isaac, and Jacob." In his words, "The heart has its reasons, which reason does not know."

Pascal's death in 1662 was followed by a period of enlightenment during which we heard from poets. According to Barrett, "Poets are witnesses to being before philosophers are able to bring it into thought. And what these particular poets were struggling to reveal were the conditions of being that are ours historically today. They were sounding, in poetic terms, the premonitory chords of our own era."[10]

We come now to the contributions of poets. Shakespeare epitomized existential thought when he had Hamlet advise his friend, "There are more things in heaven and earth, Horatio, than is dreamed of in your philosophy."[11]

Shakespeare had an astonishing ability to represent change in the characters he created. Harold Bloom observed, "Sir John Falstaff is always transforming himself, always thinking, speaking, and overhearing himself in a quicksilver metamorphosis, always willing the change and suffering the change that is Shakespeare's tribute to the reality of our lives."[12] Through his insight he created Falstaff, a totally fictitious character in three of Shakespeare's plays, whom he had create his authentic self.

Shakespeare was also in tune with later existentialists for whom mirrors symbolized the importance of self. Thus, Hamlet directs the players "to hold, as 'twere, the mirror up to nature."[13] Sartre called this process "being-for-others"—discovering ourselves as objects created by the gaze of someone else.

We have reached the time of the scientist, Isaac Newton, who contended that the underlying order that governed nature could be expressed in scientific and mathematical terms derived from observable phenomena. To this extreme rationalism, the poet William Blake responded:

> The atoms of Democritus
> And Newton's particles of light
> Are sands upon the Red Sea shore,
> Where Israel's tents do shine so bright.

In places of perfection, we find the terror and mystery of what we do not know creating uncertainties that prompted existential thinkers to ask the question, "Do things really exist or are they fictions of the mind?"[14]

William Wordsworth expressed his displeasure with philosophical reasoning, which he saw separating us from our genuine feeling about nature:

> Our meddling intellect
> Misshapes the beauteous forms of things
> We murder to dissect.

He could well have been responding to Aristotle's attempts to explain how rainbows are made when he composed this elegant metaphor: "My heart leaps up when I behold a rainbow in the sky."

For me, when I see a rainbow, I recall my first awareness of one. I was playing with my mother in our backyard when a rainbow suddenly appeared in the delicate spray of a water sprinkler. In a poetic sense, my heart leaped up even though the rainbow was not way up in the sky.

My second recollection is of a trip to Niagara Falls with my wife, Arlene, and her parents. At the base of the falls, we could see an expansive rainbow, which was only apparent from the point where we were standing. It was like the line from an Israeli pop song, "What you see from here, you don't see from there."

My third remembrance in this stream of consciousness occurred during a trip to Israel. Arlene and I were with three of my closest friends, Herb, Jason, and Marvin. It had been raining lightly, on and off, throughout the day, and rainbows seemed to be appearing almost everywhere—sometimes, several at the same time.

Each of my three friends, conditioned by his own experiences, responded to my allusion to Wordsworth differently. Herb, a physician, commented on the "heart" reference, "I never heard of a rainbow causing a tachycardia." Jason, schooled in the Bible, referred to the *bow in the clouds* after the flood as God's covenant with humankind. Marvin, a dilettante scientist, explained that the separation of colors was caused by the refraction of each color of light by the droplets of moisture in the air.

Our discussion of rainbows affords an interesting confluence of the two subjective ideas—Hungerford's "beauty is in the eye of the beholder" and the corollary "reality is in the perception of the beholder." Everyone is conditioned by a unique confluence of experiences.

Mark Twain provided an interesting fillip: "We have not the reverent feeling for the rainbow that a savage has, because we know how it is made. We have lost as much as we have gained by prying into that matter."[15]

Latin students seldom forget Rene Descartes' maxim, "Cogito ergo sum," for which the English equivalent is "I think, therefore, I am." Descartes based his philosophy on doubt. He doubted the existence of everything with the exception of his act of doubting. He reasoned that to doubt he had to think from which he inferred his existence.

To Sartre, Descartes was a hero of existential thought. His *cogito* became the kernel of Sartre's thought on two levels: the only thing Descartes could not doubt was his own existence and his capacity to say no.

The word *reality* acquired a special meaning because of Emanuel Kant's so-called Copernican revolution in philosophy. He declared that a thing in itself is not knowable by us. The word *reality* signified not that which exists in complete independence of the human mind, but only that which is knowable by and intelligible to us through our senses. His doctrine of the limitations of reason rests on the finite possibilities of human experience.

Rabbi Sherwin Wine, who kindled my interest in existentialism, put it in simpler terms. He told the story of a young lad who had never seen a donkey until he went to a circus.

In the parade of animals, he saw his first donkey, which had been painted pink. To him, all donkeys were presumed to be pink; that became his reality of the idea *donkey*. Hopefully, sometime later, the young lad became disabused of that idea.

The nineteenth century German intellectual enfant-terrible Friedrich Nietzsche provided meaningful insight along the path we are following. He was critical of idealists, from Plato onward, who set universal ideas above the psychological needs of individuals. "We cannot decide whether what we call truth is really truth or merely appears that way to us."[16]

He created Zarathustra as an idealistic type of a higher order of human, half-saint and half-genius, whom he placed on a mountaintop to meditate in solitude. Barrett explains, "Climbing a mountain is the aptest metaphor for getting above ordinary humanity. About to leave his mountain solitude, Zarathustra declares he is going down among men 'Once again to be a man.' The mountain is the solitude of the spirit; the lowlands represent the world of ordinary men."[17]

What a stroke of good fortune to discover this metaphoric mountain to bring an appropriate closure to our field trip back in time to find precursors of existential thought. Exploring the roots of existentialism, we found a second mountain of singular significance without a name and geographic location. Could Nietzsche have made his mountain more meaningful by specifying latitude and longitude? Would the reality of Sinai be enhanced if we could precisely place it on a map?

William James spoke of sitting in a symbolic armchair, quoted by Will Durant in his book *The Story of Philosophy*: "You can never know or discover truth by sitting in detachment in an armchair." Instead, he defined philosophy as only thinking about things in the most comprehensive possible way.[18]

And from the biography of William James written by Lloyd Morris: "Experience is remolding us every moment, and our mental reaction on every given thing is really a resultant of our experience of the whole world up to that date. Whatever things have intimate and continuous connection with my life are things whose reality I cannot doubt. Whatever things fail to establish this connection, are things which are practically no better for me than if they had existed not at all."[19]

Our field trip is over. We've come full circle and heard from precursors of Jean Paul Sartre, all of whom debunked previously established views. We discovered poets and playwrights who anticipated the existential philosophers. Sartre himself followed this pattern, first expressing his thoughts in fictional form prior to more formal exposition. His informal writings dealing with the human condition led to his becoming the most widely published philosopher of his time.

In his seminal novel, *Nausea*, Sartre leads the reader through the tortuous path of a search through nothingness to meaning in the form of the journal of Antoine Roquentin. His self-image is that of a dismal failure as a history researcher. In his suffering he is reduced to nothingness, to the nauseated consciousness of nothing filled with meaningless visions. He finds even his own image in a mirror detestable.

Finally, he comes to realize that his lack of ability to reflect on history is not the end of the world. He reasons that his life as a writer can become meaningful if, by his own efforts, he refines his latent talent to become an author. He feels that he has begun to discover his authentic self by going from existential failure to a potential for meaning. "I am like a man completely frozen after a trek through the snow and suddenly comes into a warm room."

Had it only been so for the Israelites liberated from slavery in Egypt. Moses sought to reach each one as an individual and so overcome their existential famine, but the cohesive force of group dynamics prohibited such a transformation. It required the emergence of a new generation to enable the people to free themselves from the shackles of slave mentality and nurture the seeds of liberty and meaning.

Sartre dealt with a comparable problem: "We have been charged with dwelling on human degradation, with pointing up everywhere the sordid, the shady and slimy and neglecting the gracious and beautiful, the bright side of human nature...by existentialism we mean a doctrine which makes human life possible and, in addition, declares that every truth and every action implies a human setting and a human subjectivity."[20]

This, indeed, is the genius of Sartre—to create a positive, constructive philosophy out of a body of thought that offered little but negation—a body of thought promulgated by large parts of the population who felt confronted with the despair and anguish of one world war and faced by the turmoil preceding another one. In his words, "A world they never made, a world too vast and complex to yield to human urging, and one which is indifferent—if not downright hostile—to human aspiration."[21]

Sartre's views are congruent with the thinking of Moses who, we will soon discover, dealt with a people consumed with similar despair and anguish. Sartre, like Moses, sought to dispel the notion of despair and hopelessness of those whose lives he touched.

In his book *Moses*, the existentialist Martin Buber addresses our question: "Whether Sinai was a volcano cannot be determined historically, nor is it historically relevant. But that the tribes gathered at the 'burning mountain,' and comprehended the words of their leader

Moses as a message of their God…is essentially an historical process."[22]

In our search for Sinai, we have completed two trips: my physical sojourn in the Negev with Shalom resulting in an existential stream of consciousness experience, and our imaginary field trip to discover precursors of existential thought. We must now proceed to look at the Exodus as Moses saw it—through an existential prism.

When white light passes through a prism, it becomes refracted so that we see the full spectrum of its visible colors like a rainbow. Light is, in a sense, spread apart by the prism. The existential prism will serve to open up the meaning of the biblical text. The triangular, wedge shape of a prism also implies that the existential process can be inserted between the lines of text to reveal the interlinear presence of God as seen through the eyes of Moses.

Rabbi Abraham Joshua Heschel paraphrased Sartre elegantly: "We are born human beings. What we must acquire is being human. Being human is the essential— the decisive—achievement of a human being."[23]

Existentialism can also have a lighter touch. It has been said an existential philosopher once pondered the bagel and asked, "Why the hole?" He concluded that the hole is the essence of the bagel—it would not be a bagel without a hole. The surrounding dough is only there to show where the hole is located.

IN THE BEGINNING
GOD WAS THERE

To understand the future relationship of Moses and God, we need to recognize how the appearance of God changed during the book of Genesis. However, despite the hiatus of four hundred years between the conclusion of Genesis and the birth of Moses in Exodus, there was a recognizable consistency in God's diminished Presence.

Skimming the Genesis highlights, we will discover an amazing change in the Presence of God. At the start, God was *in* the world, interacting with the characters. He was on center stage, so to speak.

In Richard Elliott Friedman's words: "Two crucial developments take place. The first is the diminishing of the apparent Presence of the divine among humans, the hiding of the face of God. The second, and presumably related development, is a shift in the balance of control of human destiny."[1]

God created the world in seven days and declared, "Behold, it is very good." Then, God, who created Adam and Eve, placed them in the Garden of Eden with one caveat: not to eat the fruit of the tree of knowledge, lest they die. He also gave them the existential gift of free will. Whether thirst for knowledge or to test God's resolve, they tasted the fruit and so produced God's first great disappointment.

They gave birth to two sons, Cain and Abel. When Cain killed his brother Abel, he offered the lame excuse, "Am I my brother's keeper?"

Then, in the story of the flood, we find God so distraught with the corruption on earth that he commissioned Noah to build an ark to save certain remnants of humankind and animals from a vast flood of His creation—all other living things drowned. After the deluge, God was so chagrined by His own actions that "the Lord said to Himself: 'Never again will I doom the earth because of man, since the devisings of man's mind are evil from his youth'" Genesis (8:21).

God in turn made a "never again" covenant with Noah symbolized by "my rainbow in the clouds." Do you remember the perceptions of the rainbow in chapter three is the one Jason spoke of as his first intuitive perception of a rainbow?

God was obviously faced with an existential dilemma. He created humankind, gave them freedom of choice, and now was confounded with the problem of human ambiguity including the freedom to say "no!"

Little wonder that Rabbi Saul Lieberman of the Jewish Institute of Religion challenged rabbinical students with the question, "Who is the most tragic character in the Bible?"[2] We've discussed only the first eight chapters of the Bible, and the answer is already apparent—the most tragic character in the Bible is God.

Having created the world in seven days and optimistically declared, "Behold, it is very good," he then did an about face and flooded the work of his creation.

The Tower of Babel story affords further insight into God's concerns. It speaks of an attempted effort of the people to build *a tower with its top in the sky*. The Lord personally "came down and confounded their speech, causing them to scatter over the face of the earth" (Genesis 11:3–8).

However, the meaning of God's displeasure here was not clear since their sins did not seem so egregious. It suggested that ascending to God from high places, as symbolized in ancient religions, was not what God wanted. The message was that he preferred they reach up to him through good deeds. Not adoration, but pursuit of moral grandeur was what God preferred.[3]

In these stories, God appeared as intimately involved in the affairs of the world, directly seen and heard by its inhabitants. After the Tower of Babel, the Divine Presence would never again appear among the people. He made a transition from center stage to the wings from where he gave cues to the actors onstage.

It is not unusual in the Bible to have an interlude prior to an important happening. In this case, it was the scant reference to the passing of ten generations. When the action continued, God made a stunning announcement: the Lord said to Abram, "Go forth from your native land and from your father's house to the land that I will show you. I will make of you a great nation, and I will bless you; I will make your name great, and you shall be a blessing" (Genesis 12:2).

Another twelve years, and God made a further commitment: "And you shall no longer be called Abram, but your name shall be Abraham,[a] for I make you the father of a multitude of nations... I will maintain My covenant between Me and you and your offspring to come... Such shall be the covenant... which you shall keep: every male among you shall be circumcised" (Genesis 17:6).

The covenant represented a transfer of authority and leadership, but demanded also an active response from the recipients—circumcision as a token of God's covenant and a symbol of commitment.

As the Abraham saga progressed, God absented himself from direct participation. We no longer read the words familiar in prior passages, "God came down." Instead, we see angels acting as messengers of God. The Divine Presence never again is made visible to the general public.

Another twenty-five years passed, and Abraham and his wife Sarah had their first son Isaac, the second generation in the unfolding of the covenant. Later, Isaac married Rebecca, and during that time we heard little of God. But when Rebecca was suffering from the struggling of twins in her womb, she cried out to God, "Why do I exist?" The Lord answered her, "Two nations are in your womb, two separate peoples shall issue from your body; one people shall be mightier than the other, And the older shall serve the younger" (Genesis 25:23).

---

[a]   *Abraham* taken to mean "father of a multitude."

In response, when the twins grew up, Rebecca tricked Isaac into blessing his younger son, Jacob, thereby giving him the birthright. Traditionally, the birthright should have gone to his older brother, Esau.

To Jacob, God was manifest in a different way—in dreams. God spoke to Jacob as he did to the latter's predecessors—both directly and through angels—but Jacob also experienced God in his sleep. As we well know, dreams can be confusing. Jacob's were no different.

In the first dream, angels went down and up on a stairway from heaven. And then, "the Lord was standing beside him... Jacob awoke from his sleep and said, 'Surely the Lord is in this place, and I did not know it!'" Genesis (28:16).

One would not think such juxtaposition unusual in a dream context. The following encounter, another dream sequence, was even stranger.

On his way to meet his brother Esau, Jacob spent the night by himself. *A man wrestled with him until the break of dawn.* During the struggle, he injured Jacob's hip, but Jacob would not let him go until the man blessed him.

> "Your name shall no longer be Jacob, but Israel,[b] for you have striven with beings divine and human and have prevailed. Jacob asked, 'Pray tell me your name.' But he said, 'You must not ask my name.' So Jacob named the place Peniel,

---

[b] The name, Israel, is understood to mean, "struggled with God."

meaning, "I have seen a divine being, face to face, yet my life has been preserved."'(32:29-31)

And once more, "God called to Israel in a vision by night...'I am God, the God of your father. Fear not to go down to Egypt, for I will make you there into a great nation'" (Genesis 46:2). This is a most important directive from God to Jacob, now called Israel, and again, in a dream.

There is much interest in Jacob's dreams, because they show a further stage in the separation of God from humanity's everyday business and the fusion, or confusion, of God, angels, and humans. It is confusing if we imagine angels as being separate from God when they are understood to be surrogates of God's presence.

It is also meaningful to note the importance of names in the Bible. In prebiblical tradition, the change of a name signified a status change of the individual. Hence, Abram to Abraham, Serai to Sarah[c], and Jacob to Israel to signify bestowing of the covenant. In the Jewish tradition, names are not casual designations of identity but reflection of innermost being. The relevance of names will be seen again in Exodus.

An interesting parallel to the conversation with the man in Jacob's dream will be found in Moses' first conversation with God. When Moses asks God for his name, God deigns to respond with a direct answer.

---

[c]   God changed Sarai's name to Sarah, presumably, to symbolize her change from a barren woman to one who gave birth to a future patriarch.

Our discussion of Genesis concludes with the Joseph saga. A few extracts will serve to illumine God's further lack of connection with humankind as we approach the conclusion of Genesis.

From this point on, the face of God became hidden; the transition we spoke of had been completed. God metaphorically had moved from center stage to the wings and then to a box seat. Dare we call it a sky-box? His presence was felt, but there was no direct communication between him and the players onstage.

When a word or phrase is repeated in the Bible, it warrants special attention. Thus the expression "the Lord was with Joseph," which appears four times in verse 39 is meant to emphasize the experience of God's unspoken Presence.

Prior to Joseph, Jacob had ten sons from his several wives. Joseph was his eleventh son, the first with his beloved wife Rachel. Proper parenting was not taught in those days so Jacob made no effort to conceal that he loved Joseph the best. Knowing of their father's preference for Joseph, his older brothers planned his execution.

However, rather than spill his blood, they reconsidered and abandoned him in a desert pit. He was subsequently rescued by traders who sold him to Potiphar, an Egyptian courtier of the Pharaoh.

> *The Lord was with Joseph, and he was a successful man, and he stayed in the house of his Egyptian master. And when his master saw that the Lord was with him and that the Lord lent success to everything he undertook, he took a liking to Joseph.*

He made him his personal attendant and put him in charge of his household.

Genesis (39:2–4)

"*The Lord was with Joseph*" tells us more about Joseph than about God. Joseph revealed a feeling of Divine closeness. He spoke to God, and he attributed his amazing successes to the intervention of God. Yet, in modern parlance, God never got in Joseph's face. God changed Sarai's name to Sarah, presumably, to symbolize her change from a barren woman to one who gave birth to a future patriarch.

Because of a misunderstanding about an affair with Potiphar's wife, Joseph was imprisoned. There he distinguished himself by his ability to interpret dreams. When Pharaoh learned of Joseph's amazing talent, he sent for him.

> And Pharaoh said to Joseph, "I have had a dream, but no one can interpret it. Now I have heard it said of you that for you to hear a dream is to tell its meaning." Joseph answered saying, "Not I! God will see to Pharaoh's welfare."

> Genesis 41:14-16

After an extensive explanation of the meaning of the dream, Joseph concluded with God's alleged words: "Accordingly, let Pharaoh find a man of discernment and wisdom, and set him over the land of Egypt" (Genesis 41:33–34).

Something new had been added. Clearly, Joseph was planting a seed about his own advice being the word of God. And who do you think got the job? Not only did he get the job of vizier over Egypt, but Pharaoh also changed his name. "Pharaoh then gave Joseph the name Zaphenath-paneah [Egyptian for, 'God speaks; He lives']" (Genesis 41:45).

We are prompted to question the meaning of the expression "God was with Joseph." Does it mean Joseph felt God made him bright, beautiful, and cunning to accomplish his mission? Did Joseph feel justified in exploiting the idea of *God being with him* to achieve his ambitious goals? What was Joseph thinking when he gave God the credit for interpreting Pharaoh's dream?

Such dilemmas became clearer later in the story when ten of Joseph's brothers went to Egypt hoping to procure food. It was their good fortune to appear before their brother, Joseph, who concealed the fact that he recognized them. In actuality, they had failed to recognize Joseph. Joseph insisted they return to Canaan and bring back their brother Benjamin. Before departing, Joseph had money planted in their sacks.

Upon their return, they reported the mysterious appearance of coins to Joseph's steward who, as instructed by Joseph, advised them that God must have put the treasure in their sacks. Does this obvious deception not suggest the possibility that Joseph's prior attribution of God's involvement was disingenuous?

But it's not that simple. Just as Joseph was a complicated person, so was his relation to God. In a dramatic scene in which Joseph revealed his identity to his brothers, he declared four times that it was God who brought these events to pass. The repetition in the text leaves little doubt that Joseph felt the presence of God, notwithstanding the tendency to force the issue for personal advantage.

You will identify an inherent cogency in this patchwork of Genesis. God is the common thread that binds the patches together, whether directly present or not. Skimming Genesis also presents the opportunity to visit ideas that found their way into the Bible from surrounding cultures, mostly Egyptian. Because of Moses' knowledge of Egyptian customs and theology, it will not be surprising to see these same ideas in the Grand Narrative that follows:

- ❑ Ascending to high places enabled people to get closer to deities
- ❑ The importance of names
- ❑ The relevance of dreams
- ❑ Appearance of angels as messengers of God
- ❑ Disingenuous attributions of natural events to God's intervention

The character developments of Jacob and Joseph compared to their predecessors is readily distinguishable, even in this brief synopsis. According to Friedman, "The effect of this growth is that, through the course of the first book of the Bible, the humans become more human… and become more in control of their destiny. And then comes Moses. Every aspect of this development became still more intense in the person of Moses."[4]

God as seen in the concluding chapters of Genesis, as presented by Joseph, was the same God who was with Moses. As explained by Maimonides: "It was only Moses who heard the words, and he reported them to the people."[5]

THE EDUCATION
OF A PRINCE

A new king arose over Egypt, who did not
know Joseph. And he said to his people, "Look,
the Israelite people are much too numerous for
us. Let us deal shrewdly with them, so that they
may not increase; otherwise, in the event of war,
they may join our enemies in fighting against us
and rise up from the ground.

Exodus 1:8–9

When the curtain rose on the Grand Narrative, the
scene was that of an existential famine. The Israelites
were living in robot conformity to the demented wills
of the pharaohs. For four hundred years, they had
slaved relentlessly to accommodate their vast building
programs. They baked bricks and rolled boulders from
puberty to death, without even the reprieve of a day of
rest. Under such extensive mind control, few were able
to, in Sartre's words, "discover their authentic selves."

The Egyptians ruthlessly imposed upon the
Israelites the various labors that they made

them perform. Ruthlessly, they made life bitter for them with harsh labor at mortar and bricks and with all the tasks of the field.

The king of Egypt spoke to the Hebrew midwives, one of whom was named Shiphrah and the other Puah, saying, "When you deliver the Hebrew women, look at the birthstool: if it is a boy, kill him; if it is a girl, let her live."

Exodus1:13–16

But the midwives chose to disobey the king and let boys live. Fortunately, they had the courage to rise above the existential depravity. However, Pharaoh countered their challenge with a decree that all boys born were to be thrown into the Nile and drowned.

We would not have the Grand Narrative if Moses' parents had complied. They made the deliberate existential choice to save their baby boy by hiding him for his first three months and then having his sister Miriam place him in a basket that floated to the place where Pharaoh's daughter bathed in the Nile. Maternal instinct triumphed over allegiance. She took pity on the infant and arranged to raise him as her own child.

There is a niggling question about the naming of Moses. When Pharaoh's daughter found the child, what did she call him? Some sources, including the Hebrew Bible, use the Hebrew *Moshe*, from *mashui*, meaning "drawn out," because she is said to have drawn him out of the water.

Other sources suggest she gave him the common Egyptian name, *Mose*, signifying "born of." Her choice was really a no-brainer. Can you imagine his daughter telling her father, the king of Egypt, about her newly adopted child with a nice Hebrew name like Moshe? Hardly would that have gone over well with the Pharaoh who had issued an edict to slaughter all the firstborn Hebrew male children.

The point is we need to exercise insight in interpreting the written text—even more when there is no text, as in the ensuing years. After the adoption of Mose, the curtain descended, leaving us in the dark about Mose's childhood and youth. The Bible tells us nothing more about Mose until he became a young man, presumably in his twenties.

However, since we are trying to get into Moses' head, we need to infer as much as possible about him during his formative years, the time when his name was Mose. To do so requires thoughtful speculation and envisioning what probably transpired during those early years to shape the mind of Moses.

Perhaps, as Martin Buber speculated, "The Bible simply and unabashedly fills the gaps in the transmitted biography [of Moses] by carefully drawing on the treasury of legendary motifs common to earthly humanity."[1] It is then the students' obligation to fill in the blanks from the well documented history and myths of the ancient Middle East.

In the new kingdom, childhood ended at four and was followed by formal education. The adopted son of an Egyptian princess would have been educated in the palace with other royal and upper class children.

According to Price, et al, "Mose, a prince in the court of the Pharaoh, received the intellectual training, the spiritual testing and the all-around preparation for his supreme task."[2] Education of the elite was indispensable to an official career. As described in an edifying papyrus, "Give thy heart to learning, and love her like a mother, for there is nothing so precious as learning."[3]

The ability to write was of paramount importance. Hieroglyphics, which were slow and burdensome, were replaced by a cursive style known as hieratic. Intense concern for the written word may well account for the theory that Moses contrived a script, possibly Hebrew, for the commandments and subsequent laws.

We know that Egyptian education included extensive reading, mathematics, astronomy, empirical medicine, gymnastics, swimming, and manners of the court. Such content of instruction emphasized moral precepts, many wholesome and rational, inconsistent with the practice of slavery.

Chaim Potok, in his book, *Wanderings*, wrote, "A prince would eventually have become a member of the inner circle of courtiers and would have known of wars, treaties, intrigues—the swirl of royal affairs around the divine, all powerful throne."[4] Mose might have been assigned to temporary military duty at the quarries or as an overseer of his kinfolk working on the delta.

From his military experience, we would expect that he knew of the fortifications across the Isthmus of Suez—knowledge that later enabled him to lead the Israelites across the southern portion of the isthmus where there were no military installations. He would have spent sufficient time with the Egyptian troops in the desert so as to become familiar with its geography and know where wells and oases were available.

James Henry Breasted, a recognized authority, described the foods of the noble and official classes as rich and varied: "ten different kinds of meat, five kinds of poultry, sixteen types of bread and cakes, six different wines, four varieties of beer, eleven fruits, besides all sorts of sweets."[5]

Pigs were considered filthy animals, unfit to be eaten because they were alleged to copulate under a full moon. In neighboring Babylonia, although swine's flesh was considered unclean, it could be offered to evil demons. It might well be that pork prejudice was due to the fact that pigs, unlike other edible animals, ate human food in competition for the food supply.

The Egyptian menu gives us a clue as to the possible origin of the foods proscribed in Leviticus, the laws of *kashrut*—foods not on the menu were not known to Mose as being safe to eat. Pork was a special case, suggesting why, to this day, even the most casual observers of the dietary laws avoid pork, if nothing else.

Pharaoh's military storehouse was filled with elaborately wrought chariots, weapons, whips, and gold mounted staffs, while his stalls boasted fine horses and cattle. The houses of the rich were filled with the most exquisite products of the Asiatic craftsmen and artists.

The building program of Pharaoh Ramses I, Mose's adopted grandfather, "was on a scale surpassing in size and extent anything that his ancestors had ever accomplished…the obelisks which he erected… arose among his temples."[6] Today, we might conceptualize this as a huge Federal Construction Project, unfortunately concentrated on palaces for the rich rather than low cost housing.

In his book *Our Oriental Heritage*, Will Durant sets the stage for the Exodus accordingly: "There is probably little question of the correctness of the Hebrew tradition in attributing the oppression of some tribes of their ancestors to the building of Pithom and Ramses. That a tribe of their forefathers should have fled the country to escape such labor is quite in accord with what we know of the time."[7]

The laws, which Moses later promulgated to maintain order among the Israelites were not derived in a vacuum. He would have studied those of the Hammurabi, the Assyrians, and the Hittites and would have been thoroughly conversant with the Egyptian Book of the Dead.

Comparisons convince us that the laws of the Torah have many points in common with earlier codes, but the intent is not the same. The laws of the Bible are essentially religious while those Mose studied were primarily civil. For the most part, Egyptian religion had little to say about morality.

There can be little doubt that Mose was impressed with the theological ideas of the Pharaoh Ikhnaton who reigned for a short period about 130 years earlier. Will Durant tells us that, "Iknaton's youthful spirit rebelled against the sordidness into which the religion of the people had fallen; he abominated the indecent wealth and lavish ritual of the temples...he announced bravely that all these rods and ceremonies were a vulgar idolatry, that there was but one god—Aton."[8]

To Ikhnaton, the single invisible deity Aton was the creative and nourishing heat of the sun's invisible rays. His attempted revolution to abolish all other deities failed after seventeen years because of his impatience. He tried to force too rapid replacement of superstitious polytheism with a monotheism requiring imagination and intelligence.

Ikhnaton was on the right track, but he didn't get it right. The idea of worshipping the rays of the sun, which would provide warmth and light during the day but leave the nights dark and cold, was a tough sell at best. He was also too impulsive, expecting to revolutionize religious practice within a seventeen-year window—forty might have worked better. "Forty" is a biblical idiom, as seen in the duration of the flood and the subsequent desert wanderings, meant to convey a long time.

Following the reign of Ikhnaton, Egyptian culture reverted to that of his predecessors. The Hebrew word for Egypt, *Mitsrayim*—whose root *matsar* means narrow, limited, or restricted—presents an interesting parallel between the geography and the culture. The habitable portion of Egypt was narrow, no more than thirty miles wide. The narrowness of their ideas, such as idol worship, multiple deities, and slavery would have been an abomination to someone of a more complicated intellect and sensitivity such as Mose.

Apparently, Ikhnaton's idea of an invisible god gave Mose food for thought. It's unlikely he learned anything about the God of Abraham from his kinfolk who were separated from Joseph by four hundred years and had acquired what little they knew about theology from their Egyptian neighbors. Ikhnaton's ideas might have provided his first exposure to the idea of a single, invisible god.

When the curtain goes back up after the hiatus of our conjecture, the scene was described as follows:

> Sometime after that, when Moses had grown up, he went out to his kinfolk and witnessed their labors. He saw an Egyptian beating a Hebrew, one of his kinsmen. He looked this way and that and, seeing no one about, he struck down the Egyptian and hid him in the sand. When he went out the next day, he found two Hebrews fighting; so he said to the offender, "Why do you strike your fellow?" He retorted, "Who made you chief and ruler over us? Do you mean to kill me as you killed the Egyptian?"
>
> Exodus 2:11–14

In both cases, Mose acted in outrage of injustice—in neither case for self protection or personal satisfaction. In the first, out of concern for a kinsman and, in the latter, to protect one Hebrew from another; both instances reveal his unbiased indignation of brutality.

The comment of the Hebrew suggests that the probable act of manslaughter was known, so Mose realized he had to deal with it. The Bible relates that Pharaoh intended to kill him.

This passage presents an intriguing question. The writer would have us believe it was fear of Pharaoh's reprisal that prompted Mose to take to the desert. On the other hand, we need to consider the likelihood that Mose did not fear the wrath of his adopted grandfather. If the relationship of grandfather to grandson was as we know it, Mose would have sensed that if he proffered an explanation the worst that might have happened would have been a mild reproach because for the Egyptians human life was expendable.

Legends are replete about Mose's anguish over the Hebrew's suffering. Consider these apocryphal statements attributed to him: "Woe is me for your servitude! Would that I could die for you! ...Wherein has Israel sinned that they should be enslaved more than any other nation?"[9]

The many commentaries expressing Mose's suffering over the plight of the Hebrews portend the killing of the Egyptian. It was not done as a result of momentary rage, but as a response to meditations of the heart. Whether he acted peremptorily or not is unimportant. The abuse of the slave was not unusual—he had probably witnessed the same scene countless times.

After the fact, Mose must have reflected on why he had so acted this time. Was it to save the life of a Hebrew? Was he making a statement to provoke Pharaoh? Or was he trying to assuage his own conscience?

It is difficult to believe he was faced with a life or death decision; instead, he was faced with a huge existential choice—actually one of three:

- ❑ He could take off into the wilderness.
- ❑ He could explain and not complain.
- ❑ He could do nothing—existentially, doing nothing is a choice.

He summarily rejected the possibility of reforming Pharaoh, his grandfather, whose paramount concern was the building project, which was contingent on cheap labor. Mose knew that was not a viable option.

Had he elected to stay, he would then live in the lap of a degree of luxury unknown anywhere else in the world. The appeal of that lifestyle can be seen by a visit to contemporary Egypt or museum displays of the splendors of the ancient world. Further, he would have become a major figure in the royal court.

We must imagine him relinquishing sleeping on Egyptian cotton sheets for a bed of hot desert sand with blistering sun by day and painful cold at night. Life in the wilderness was not something Mose only conceptualized; he had actually been there.

However, he also had to live with himself and his own conscience. Since he knew, as a member of the court, he could do little to benefit his kinfolk, he could no longer endure the guilt and anguish of his present predicament. Moses became aware of his existential "authentic self" and departed from the court, which can be characterized as an act of "righteous indignation," a favorite expression of my friend and rabbi, Richard C. Hertz.

RIGHTEOUS
INDIGNATION

*Moses fled from Pharaoh. He arrived in the land of
Midian, and sat down beside a well.*

Exodus 2:15

The Bible presents this momentous event in an off-hand manner, as if he had just gone around the corner for a cup of goat's milk, failing to mention an interval of years.

Although the narrator treated it perfunctorily, Moses had made a monumental decision to depart from Egypt—an existential choice that ultimately would change the course of human history. But first, he could now change his name from Mose to Moses.

He did not travel to Canaan, the roots of his kinfolk, because Egyptian troops were stationed there. Instead, he went southeast to the wilderness of Sinai and wandered into the land of Midian, the region now known as Elat, south of modern Israel.

We cannot take biblical years and ages literally; the implication was Moses spent most of his adult life, about sixty years, in Midian. Since biblical interpretation takes the frequently used expression "forty years" as a long time, sixty years must have meant a very long time.

Later events reveal that as leader of the Hebrews he was knowledgeable of desert geography and survival, indicating experience beyond that acquired as a youth in Pharaoh's military. Even if he had traveled by camel—unlikely—the time involved between leaving Egypt and arriving in Midian would have been years.

He learned how to live with blistering daytime sun and bitter nighttime cold. He knew where to find water, where there were impassable barriers, and where Egyptian fortifications were located.

Knowledge of the natural phenomena, among them those later called plagues, was no mystery to him. He would have experienced them first hand. He would also have learned how to safely cross the Sea of Reeds, often erroneously referred to as the Red Sea.

Finally, Moses arrived at the well at which point the narrative continues: "Now the priest of Midian had seven daughters. They came to draw water, and filled their troughs to water their father's flock; but shepherds came and drove them off. Moses rose to their defense, and he watered their flock (Exodus 2:16–17).

Perhaps there is a cogent explanation for the leap in the Bible from Moses' departure from Egypt to the scene at the well. It may have been to conjoin the confrontations with the Egyptian and that of the shepherds. The narrator may have been more concerned with the character of Moses, his inspiration to champion justice, than with his learning curve. It is significant to note that no mention was made of his receiving the message to leave Egypt from God.

When the seven daughters returned to their father Reuel, also known as Jethro, they explained that an Egyptian had rescued them. Reuel had them invite Moses to break bread and stay with them.

Moses later married Jethro's daughter, Zipporah, who bore a son named Gershom—the name meaning "a stranger there," with *there* not being Midian. Was Moses thinking of returning to Egypt where his son would have been a stranger?

The Midianites were a peaceful desert folk of enterprising shepherds and traders. For Moses they represented a simple way of life and a stern moral code, in sharp contrast to the hedonistic polytheism of Egypt. They knew nothing of the Egyptian obsession with funerary rituals, cult of the dead, or exploitation of slaves.

It is alleged that Jethro was in some way descended from Abraham and was familiar with the God of the Genesis family. If so, Jethro probably gave Moses a different slant on the idea of one God than that of Ikhnaton, of a God you could not see, but who saw you.

Jethro was highly intelligent and enlightened, so it is likely the two spent many evenings together exchanging ideas. Moses was able to explain mathematics, astronomy, and Egyptian law and customs. His father-in-law might have taught Moses leadership, desert survival, sheep herding, and the destruction of idols. The latter idea might have been passed along from Abraham, his progenitor of many generations.

All the Bible tells us about Egypt during the ensuing years is that the king had died and that God heard and responded to the groaning of the Israelites in bondage. The Bible speaks of the period as *a long time*. No mention was made that during that same time Moses tended Jethro's sheep and nurtured his own family.

Vanished were the days of life in an Egyptian palace, the rich, black soil of the Nile valley, and the vast temples. In their place were the hot dry sand and scalding sun with nowhere to rest while he watched Jethro's flock search for sparse leaves and a few blades of grass.

Surely, he recalled the Hebrew slaves, who, resembling the sheep he tended, were herded like cattle. Could he have conceived of tending sheep as a metaphor for what might someday be his calling to shepherd the Israelites across these same sands?

A familiar *midrash* eloquently embellishes the metaphor:

> When Moses was tending Jethro's flock in the wilderness, a lamb scampered off until it approached a shelter under a rock. As the lamb reached the shelter it came upon a pool of water and stopped to drink. When Moses caught up with it he said, "I did not know you ran away because you were thirsty. Now you must be tired." So he hoisted the lamb on his shoulders and started walking back with it. The Holy One said, "Because you showed such compassion in tending the flock of a mortal, as you live you

shall become shepherd of Israel, the flock that is Mine."[1]

We can only speculate as to what Moses thought about during those years alone while tending sheep. But wonder we must since getting into Moses' head is our objective.

Undoubtedly, he thought about the death of the Egyptian—not his murder, because that was not intended. He had reacted in a sudden burst of uncontrollable rage, not intending to kill him. But think about the guilt he must have felt. To an Egyptian, a most ignominious death would have been burial in the sand without proper funereal rites.

Also foremost in his mind must have been his concern for the Hebrews who were still suffering under the lashes of their cruel taskmasters. Such concern was indelibly etched on his mind and never far removed from his consciousness.

Even if I were wrong about the compassion Pharaoh, his adopted grandfather, might have felt for him, that king was now dead. Egyptian law granted amnesty to those who had committed misdeeds during the reign of a deceased ruler. So whatever the reason for leaving Egypt, Moses knew he could now return with impunity.

Whether he left Egypt because he had to or chose to, he departed with a feeling of "righteous indignation"—Rabbi Hertz's phrase expressing a God-inspired response to an unjust or unworthy act. He asserted that it didn't matter if the responder felt inspired or thought it was an act of reason; such feelings came from the Lord.

Chaim Potok assumed the freedom of the novelist to extract these thoughts from the mind of Moses:

> The feeling that slavery is wrong could only have come from a god. What god? Certainly not the gods of Egypt. A Canaanite god? A new god then. A god who so detests Egypt that he will implant in a man the impulse to kill Egyptians on his behalf.
>
> Where is that god? How is he to be called? And why has he chosen me as the instrument of his action? Clearly Egypt is eyes—her preoccupation with death and tombs, her vast temples, her multitude of gods. He must be a god of life if he so abominates death; he must be a god of freedom if he so abominates slavery. But what is his name?[2]

This is the point at which Moses' mind might have come upon a moment of luminous awareness. The deep and abiding concern for his people had come into sharp focus as his reason for being. But what could he—a humble Bedouin in desert garb—do? Rabbi Abba Hillel Silver had the same question in mind: "How Moses came to entertain his revolutionary ideas is no greater mystery than the revolutionary insights that come to all men of genius."[3]

Moses must have reasoned that acting alone he wouldn't have a chance. Horrible as the suffering of the Hebrews was, there was no way he could appear before them and make them an offer they couldn't refuse, like saying, "Stick with me, brothers, and I'll get you out of this horrible mess!"

Nor could he demand of the present Pharaoh, "Be a *mensch* and let the slaves go free. What you have been doing resonates as the embodiment of evil!"

However, the Hebrews and Pharaoh might respond affirmatively if his words were presented as a response to commands from a higher authority, one they could be taught to relate to. They all knew and feared gods.

The enlistment of Egyptian deities wouldn't work. For too long they had been known to tolerate slavery to be of any credibility. Besides, as a matter of personal integrity, he couldn't presume to speak for gods he never believed existed.

Why not the invisible God of whom Jethro had spoken, the God who spoke to Abraham? To him slavery would have been an abomination and the freedom of humankind an imperative. He, Moses, commissioned by that God, could solicit consideration from Pharaoh and command the serious attention of the Hebrew slaves.

It is a mystery how a new and wondrous light can suddenly illumine the mind of man and create a vision of the future. We can gain insight about such a process from the words of Mozart, another supremely creative genius: "Whence and how my ideas come I know not; nor can I force them." And Heschel's comment, "The source of the prophet's utterances is his own mind. Moses' prophetic career may be traced back directly to spiritual curiosity."[4]

These thoughts engender questions each of us must ponder, because they lead to the answer to the fundamental question of how Moses considered God. Did Moses feel himself summoned and given a mission (revelation)? Did he call upon the God of Abraham for guidance (inspiration)? Or did he, himself, conceive the idea of God as the source of the mission (cognition)?

Our knowledge so far has been mostly hypothetical and too sparse for an assured conclusion. It took Moses, a certifiable genius, a year to come to a conclusion. Unless your background exceeds that of an annual Passover seder, don't even try to resolve the question now—further acquaintance with the Grand Narrative will help us to reach more solid ground.

On the other hand, should you have a prior conviction—fundamentalism, humanism, or something in between—viewing the Exodus through the mind of Moses may enrich that perspective.

Richard C. Hertz, Rabbi of Temple Beth El,
1953-1982, was an ardent advocate of
"Righteous Indignation" and interfaith relations.

THE GRAND ENCOUNTER

I n its typical laconic style, the Bible takes us from the sands of the desert to the mountain Horeb, a name connoting desolate wasteland. There was no fanfare, no exalted poetry to introduce the meeting of the One, eternal God of Israel and the towering personality of Moses. We read only these simple words: "Now Moses, tending the flock of his Father-in-law Jethro, the priest of Midian, drove the flock into the wilderness, and came to Horeb, the mountain of God" (Exodus 3:1).

Despite the absence of glorious rhetoric, the narrator tells us what he wants us to know. From this brief passage we learn that Moses was alone in what will soon be the presence of God—no one there to take notes. But why is this scrubby place called the mountain of God?

The mystery was apparently intended for those to whom Moses would relate the story. The Israelites were familiar with mountaintops as the divine seats of the bewildering mass of Egyptian deities, and so the initial appearance of the God of Israel on a high place would be in keeping with Egyptian custom. Location would contribute to the authenticity of the event. The scrubby mountainside suggests that God can be experienced anywhere.

> "A bush all aflame, yet the bush was not consumed"
>
> Exodus 3:2

Fire, because of its nonmaterial, formless, luminous qualities, was another object of religious awe from primitive man on. The Egyptians used fire to make sacrifices to their deities, but those fires self-extinguished. The only exception was Aton, the sun god, but the sun was distant and even vanished at night.

Here was an amazing fire from which an angel and then God spoke directly to Moses. The familiar elements of mountain and fire would certainly get the attention of the Israelites.

> God called to him out of the bush: "Moses! Moses!" He answered, "Here I am." And He Said, "Do not come closer. Remove the sandals from your feet, for the place on which you stand is holy ground. *I am*." He said, "The God of your father, the God of Abraham, the God of Isaac, and the God of Jacob." And Moses hid his face, for he was afraid to look at God.
>
> Exodus 3:4–6

Why did God command Moses to remove his sandals? The ground was hot sand imbedded with stones; it would have been like walking on hot coals.

However, it was a sign of respect and humility in the ancient near east to remove one's shoes when entering a religious place. God was reinforcing still another custom familiar to residents of Egypt.

The words *I am*, a solemn, self-identifying mode of address introducing royal proclamations and inscriptions would also be familiar to the Egyptians and their slaves, lending additional weight to any pronouncement.

At that time, the word *holy* had a specific meaning different from our present understanding. The Hebrew word for *holy* (*kadosh*) was derived from an Akkadian root meaning separation. *Holy* appeared only once before in the Bible (Genesis 2:3) relating to the seventh day, the day God rested after the six days of creation. It conveyed the sense of being separated in time from the preceding six days.

In the bush incident, there was a separation of space because God's presence created an aura of awe, mystery, and wonder within His proximity. As such, the space of crusty, sandy soil surrounding the bush took on a numinous quality.

This was the beginning of a change in the perception of Holiness from an objective to a subjective value. Moses sought to transform the concept for, as Rudolph Otto explained, "the sublime and the Holy becoming firmly established and carried on into the highest forms of religious consciousness."[1]

"The God of your father," an expression carried over from Genesis, is intended to emphasize continuity. All were to know that the invisible God who manifested himself here was also the God of Moses' antecedents.

The epithet "God of the father" is not unique to the Bible. It is documented in the ancient Near East as far back as the nineteenth century BCE. The expression is clearly another effort to establish connections with the past.

"The God of Abraham, the God of Isaac, and the God of Jacob." Do you wonder why this was not simply stated as the God of Abraham, Isaac, and Jacob? In the chapter discussing Genesis, each of the patriarchs experienced God in a different way. Although God was understood to be constant, each one experienced God differently and arrived at his own unique perception of the deity.

Are you beginning to see a pattern developing? The conventional wisdom is that God's words were only for Moses, and certainly, a good case can be made for that. But through the existential prism we see an effort to link past experiences to the reality of the invisible God. God spoke directly to Moses, but appeared to be speaking through Moses to the world of Moses.

> And the Lord continued, "I have marked well the plight of My people in Egypt and have heeded their outcry....I have come down to rescue them from the Egyptians and to bring them out of that land to a good and spacious land, a land flowing with milk and honey.
>
> Exodus 3:7–8

God defined himself as the God of my people in Egypt, the people who had cried out to Him for help. He had *come down*, seemingly from on high—a familiar anthropomorphic figure of speech expressing the caring love relationship of a deity.

The Israelites would need ample incentive to accept release from their confining—but familiar—habitat and paltry diet to spaciousness and ample nutrition, *a land flowing with milk and honey.* The insight shows recognition of the culture shock slaves would have breaking away from their bondage. They would have to part from the known, no matter how intolerable, for the uncertainty of the unknown.

> I will send you to Pharaoh, and you shall free My people, the Israelites, from Egypt... But Moses said to God, "Who am I that I should go to Pharaoh and free the Israelites from Egypt?" And He said, "I will be with you; that shall be your sign that it was I who sent you. And when you have freed the people from Egypt, you shall worship God at this mountain."
>
> 3:10–12

Was Moses' question "Who am I...?" an expression of humility and unworthiness, or was it Moses calling on God to make clear that he, Moses, had been delegated by a higher authority and was not acting of his own volition?

Next, Moses asked God how to respond when the Israelites asked if he had a name. This request relates to our discussion in the Genesis chapter about the importance of names. Umberto Cassuto explains, "According to the conception prevailing in the ancient East, the designation of any entity was to be equated with its existence: whatever is without an appellation does not exist, but whatever has a denomination has existence."[2]

It would be of paramount importance to the Israelites for the invisible God to have a name to verify his existence, as Moses, who thought along Egyptian lines, understood.

> Moses said to God, "When I come to the Israelites and say to them 'The God of your fathers has sent me to you,' and they ask me, 'What is His name?' what shall I say to them?" And God said to Moses, "EHYEH-ASHER-EHYEH (I WILL BE WHAT I WILL BE)... This shall be my name forever. This is my appellation for all eternity.
>
> Exodus 3:13–15

In the text that follows, not once does Moses question the meaning of these words. To him, the idea that God stated his name as "I will be what I will be," strange as it sounds, was neither enigmatic nor troubling. It was clear, as Samuel Terrien explained, "the name carried the connotation of divine Presence, but it also conferred upon this Presence a quality of elusiveness,"[3] a quality real, but unseen. Further, Moses understood its existential implications.

Moses seemed to know intuitively, as Karl Jaspers did three thousand years later, that "Only in ways that man can grasp does the Deity appear. Being can not be thought, it can only be encountered."[4] In existential terms, reality is in the eye of the beholder.

Jaspers hit the nail on the head. We encounter God as we experience His Presence—another way of saying, "I will be what I will be." The possible manifestations of God are virtually limitless, but humans are limited by the extent of our experiences as to what we are able to perceive.

A modification of Jasper's statement might help to better explain it. Only in ways that humans can grasp can gravity be understood. Newton wrote an equation to scientifically affirm that gravity exists, but if an apple fell and whacked you on the head, you'd get the message quickly. Yet even such a simple experience could be perceived in different ways—apples and apple trees are not all the same and one's head covering can make a difference.

Hence, the Deity will be that which the Israelites will be able to perceive—"will be" because as they acquire new experiences, their perceptions will become enriched. To them, the perception of God would always be in a state of becoming. Nehama Liebowitz explained it as "the existential present and henceforth."[5]

This progressive process is described by Babya in a Torah commentary: "Man must gradually train his intellectual powers to achieve the perception of the Divine... not all at once but 'as the dawn slowly but surely turns to sunrise.'"[6]

Moses made it look easy. But for years prior to the existential movement, scholars struggled with the meaning of God's concise, three-word name. In contemporary parlance, a less precise translation such as, "I will be what the mind already knows," would seem more illuminating.

Sartre was familiar with the idea of becoming for he was a novelist before becoming a philosopher and said anecdotally what he later presented formally. In his novel *Nausea*, he made this observation: "If I were ever to go on a trip, I think I should have written notes of the slightest traits of my character before leaving, so that when I returned I would be able to compare what I was and what I had become."[7]

While Moses understood the implications of God's self-naming, he also knew how daunting the task would be to convey the idea of the invisible God to the Israelites whose lives were limited to an existential vacuum in which deities were depicted as physical personifications of nature residing on mountaintops.

Moses ingeniously thought it would be possible relate certain experiences the Israelites might encounter as manifestations of God—a process of conditioned perceptions. Even when experienced collectively, each individual would have to think of them as unique, personal, and private extensions of what their minds already knew.

Coupled with the problem of leading the slaves, of whatever number, from Israel to Canaan would be that of cultivating the fulfillment of each individual by finding a place in the world through moving from baking bricks to baking cakes. "He continued, 'Thus shall you say to the Israelites, "EHYEH sent me to you"' (Exodus 3:14).

The discussion of the name may seem excessive, but its meaning is so germane to getting into Moses' head that the issue needs to be abundantly clear. For our purpose, the implicit concept is actually the glue that binds the Grand Narrative together. It's indispensable to an understanding of how Moses thought to make the Exodus successful. However, if the meaning of *EHYEH* is not yet crystal clear, any ambiguity will vanish during the ensuing journey.

However, an obvious question requires prompt attention. The verb *EHYEH* looks and sounds like it spawned a word often used for God, Yahveh, and the four-letter symbol for God, YHVH.

There are a multitude of explanations, but one that seems most plausible is from Samuel Terrien. In his book *The Elusive Presence*, He explained that at the time of Moses the name would not have been written; the oral predecessor of *EHYEH* was primitively *hawah*, very close to the Tetragramation, *YHVH*, in Hebrew,[8]. יהוה The Etymological Dictionary of the Hebrew Language offers considerably more insight on this subject.[9]

In Jewish practice, the spoken word *Adonai* is substituted for YHVH in deference to the ultimate sanctity of God's name. In other circles, however, it is often pronounced Yahveh or Jehovah.

God told Moses to tell *the elders of Israel* that *the God of your fathers* had appeared to him; the message being that God needed Moses to get himself into the world and to help rescue them from *Egyptian oppression*. God assured Moses they would listen to Him. Then, on their behalf, Moses would go to the king of Egypt and say to him:

The Lord, the God of the Hebrews, manifested Himself to us. Now, therefore, let us go a distance of three days into the wilderness to sacrifice to the Lord our God." Yet I know that the king of Egypt will let you go only because of a greater might. So I will stretch out My hand and smite Egypt with various wonders which I will work upon them; after that he will let you go.

Exodus 3:18–20

Moses replied, "What if they do not believe me?" To demonstrate how to impress the Pharaoh, God turned Moses' rod into a snake and back into a rod. Then, God covered Moses' hand with snowy scales and, as if by magic, caused the scales to disappear.

One must recognize the importance of magic in Egyptian culture. Ikhnaton, more than one hundred years prior to Moses, attempted to expunge it from religious practice but to no avail, for it was too deeply imbedded in their customs. Hence, Moses would have to demonstrate to the present Pharaoh his facility in the arcane art of magic to establish his credibility.

The rod to snake trick was standard magic with the Egyptian priests. Like all such illusions, there is an undisclosed explanation. Indigenous to the area was a type of cobra that could be stiff as a rod but, when thrown on the ground, coiled and slithered. Then, when slung by the tail, it became rigid again. Obvious care must be taken to make sure one has the right kind of snake, and it is significant that Moses didn't ask— he knew.

The hand trick was more subtle. The appearance was that of magically causing leprosy—a disease dreaded by the Egyptians—to appear and disappear. It so happens there is an exfoliate dermatitis, which resembles leprosy that can be quickly cured by exposure to the sun. My good friend, dermatologist Dr. Colman Mopper, offered this hypothesis.

Moses expressed a further reservation, that he was *slow of speech*. The Lord responded with the assurance that he would be with Moses and instruct him what to say.

Moses objected again, "Please, O Lord, make someone else your agent." This plea annoyed God who, then, declared that Moses was to be accompanied by his brother, Aaron.

> You shall speak to him and put the words in his mouth—I will be with you and with him as you speak, and tell both of you what to do—and he shall speak for you to the people. Thus he shall serve as your spokesman, with you playing the role of God to him.
>
> Exodus 4:14–16

Moses' lack of self-confidence seems incongruous with the persona we have seen. Is this the Moses, the giant of history, of whom Henry George said, "From between the paws of the rock-hewn sphinx rises the genius of human liberty and trumpets of the Exodus throb with the defiant proclamation of the rights of man? With whom among the founders of empires shall we compare him?"[10]

Something strange was happening. Moses objected three times, and each time, God's assuring words were "I will be with you." All we know of the dialogue is what Moses reported. Why, then, since Moses was to bear the burden of leadership, would he recount his doubts and lack of self-assurance only to be reassured three times?

Moses' major concern was to make clear to the Israelites that the mission was God's will, not his idea. It was God who was committed to lead them from servitude to freedom. It was not because of Moses' apparent arrogance or desire for authority, but despite his inadequacies that God chose Moses, a humble, God-fearing man. Most importantly, the Israelites must know YHVH would always be with them.

God defined the difficulties of the twofold challenge. With God's oversight and Aaron at his side, Moses was commissioned to persuade Pharaoh to release the Israelites from bondage and to convince the Israelites to follow him. The latter task would ultimately prove to be more difficult than the former.

I recall a metaphorical poem about a butterfly. It began with the line, "Oh, how I would love to fly." The butterfly, then, proceeded to contemplate how comfortable he felt ensconced in a cocoon. He went on, at some length, to extol the peaceful security of maintaining the status quo.

The poem concluded with a repetition of the opening line, "Oh, how I would love to fly," to which the poet responded, "But not until you get rid of the cocoon." This response implies butterflies had freedom of choice, but if they wanted to flee or fly, they had to exercise that choice and expose themselves to the unknown.

The Israelites were free to choose, but it would take a lot of persuasion. Sartre said that to choose implied also the right to say no.

Moses' encounter with God concluded in the same matter of fact manner as it began: "And take with you the rod, with which you shall perform the signs" (Exodus 4:17).

The Grand Encounter brings into focus the question discussed before, "where did the words come from?" In a literal sense, Moses appeared to have experienced a revelation; however, the opposite choice would be that the dialogue was a creation of Moses' own mind. Anything in between would have been an inspiration. Each of us is free to choose.

In all your ways know Him.

Proverbs 3:6

SHOW TIME

The narrator of Exodus, so inclined to brevity, approached Moses' coming negotiations with Pharaoh with a much broader brush than the biblical chapter of the Grand Encounter. Meetings with the Pharaoh filled seven chapters. The writer did have a sense of drama after all.

On the other hand, Chaim Potok, in *Wanderings*, was more succinct about these events:

> When it came time to put into final literary form the nature of events that made possible the slave escape—something of a chaotic nature of events must have occurred in Egypt for the escape to have succeeded—it was written that the Nile turned to blood; frogs, vermin and wild beasts swarmed over the land; boils afflicted men and beasts; animals and crops were destroyed; the sun no longer shone; first born were slain. A multitude of slaves made good their escape into the Red Land.[1]

> However, Potok missed the most important point of all—in a new light, God was there. The curtain rises as God, through Moses, intervened in the course of human history. Drama aside,

that alone would have justified expanding the details.

> Then Moses and Aaron went and assembled all the elders of the Israelites. Aaron repeated all the words the Lord had spoken to Moses, and he performed the sign in the sight of the people. And the people were convinced. When they heard that the Lord had taken note of the Israelites and that He had seen their plight, they bowed low in homage.
>
> Exodus 4:29–31

The first directive given in the encounter had been completed. The signs, the explanation of the name YHVH, and details of the dialogue convinced the Israelites to respect the Lord's commitment and adhere to the orders of Moses and Aaron.

> Afterwards Moses and Aaron went and said to Pharaoh, "Thus says the Lord, the God of Israel: 'Let My people go that they may celebrate a festival for Me in the wilderness.'"
>
> Exodus 5:1

Picture this bizarre sight. Standing before the throne of the King of Egypt was a wanderer, with the dust of the desert still on his sandals, and a miserable slave. By what authority did they gain admittance to the great Ramses II?

A logical explanation was Moses' relationship; after all, the new Pharaoh was his uncle. Moses' admittance gave credence to his stand as a member of the royal court during the reign of Ramses I, his adopted grandfather. Quite likely, his uncle was interested in what Moses had been doing and whether he might want to return as a functionary in the court.

Imagine Pharaoh's surprise when, after some polite talk, the conversation turned to the subject of a God he had never heard of who wanted those who served him to take a few days off. This reaction would have been anticipated: "Who is the Lord that I should heed Him and let Israel go? I do not know the Lord, nor will I let Israel go" (Exodus 5:2).

On the other hand, Pharaoh surprisingly played the punishment card by inflicting greater hardships on the Israelites. He mandated they produce the same quota of bricks as before but now without straw.

He deliberately chose not to chastise Moses and Aaron without knowing more about their alleged God. He knew how clever Moses was. It could have been a ploy because of Moses' ingenuity; but he had to be cautious considering that it might be a fearsome reality. The Egyptians knew better than to take chances with gods.

Word came back to Moses that the foreman of the Israelites had beseeched God to punish Moses for making them seem loathsome to Pharaoh.

When Moses spoke to God of his dilemma, God told him to say to the Israelites that He would free them from their labors, they might become His people, and they should be cognizant that He was their God. But their spirits had been crushed, and they ignored Moses' words.

The Lord knew the continuing confrontation with Pharaoh would wreak increasing hardships, but his immediate concern was to reveal His presence to the Israelites and make the importance of their freedom more compelling.

Then the Lord told Moses to tell Pharaoh to let the Israelites depart from the land. Moses was eighty years old and Aaron eighty-three when they made their demands on Pharaoh. Considering the narrator's paucity of detail, why were the ages of the brothers important? Aside from the obvious point that it meant they were old, we should consider the possibility that the intention was to convey Pharaoh and Moses were about the same age. It would be difficult to assume Ramses II was much older.

Being about the same age and residents of the court, they would have gone to school together, which further explains Moses' ease of access. If Ramses II had been perceptive, he would have recognized that Moses' brain was gloriously different.

In the presence of Pharaoh, Aaron cast down his rod, and it worked. But the Egyptian magicians did the same thing. However, Aaron's serpent swallowed their serpents. Yet Pharaoh's heart stiffened. He was still obsessed with the building project inherited from his father requiring vast labor resources. It seemed nothing could deter him from this compulsion.

The drama intensifies:

> And the Lord said to Moses, "Say to Aaron: Take your rod and hold out your arm over the waters of Egypt... that they may turn to

blood"... and all the water of the Nile turned into blood [the first of the ten plagues]. But when the Egyptian magicians cast the same spells, Pharaoh's heart stiffened and he paid no regard, even to this.

Exodus 7:19–22

After another seven days the Lord instructed Moses and Aaron to go to Pharaoh and tell him that if you continue to you hold God's people hostage He will plague Egypt with frogs

Pharaoh was recalcitrant to God's entreaty, and so frogs came up and covered the land. Once again the magicians tried to work their spell but this time without success. Pharaoh then called upon Moses and Aaron to remove the frogs, offering to let the people go to sacrifice to the Lord. But when the frogs retreated, he reneged on his offer.

And so it continued during seven more plagues. Although the magicians were no longer in the picture, the scenarios were similar. Each time Pharaoh would appear to acquiesce and proffer freedom, but when relief was in sight, he would become obdurate and break his word.

These were the nine natural plagues:

1. Nile turned to blood
2. Frogs
3. Lice
4. Insects
5. Pestilence
6. Boils

7. Hail
8. Locusts
9. Darkness

Arguably, the plagues were of increasing severity; but the ninth, darkness, made the greatest impression.

> Then the Lord said to Moses, "Hold out your arm toward the sky that there may be darkness upon the face of the land of Egypt, a darkness that can be touched." Moses held out his arm toward the sky and thick darkness descended upon the land of Egypt for three days... but all the Israelites enjoyed light in their dwellings.
>
> Exodus 10:21–23

Here, the Lord addressed only Moses, not Moses and Aaron collectively. This inconsistency occurs several times during the drama, with Aaron sometimes present and at other times not. According to my teacher Rabbi Daniel Polish, It appears that Aaron's presences might have been grafted on by a later writer.

Do you think the plagues were miracles? Moses certainly intended they were to appear as such. He knew that reality would be in the eyes of the beholders. That not withstanding, the above nine can be explained as consistent with the vicissitudes of nature occurring in the Nile Valley. Greta Hört, a German scholar and educator, propounded a plausible theory relating the nature and sequence of these events to uncommonly heavy rainfall in the region.[2]

Gary Greenberg posited the observation in, Myths in the Bible, that a remarkably similar description of the series of events was found in an ancient Egyptian papyrus (circa 2200 BCE), "Admonitions of an Egyptian Sage."[3]

Hört describes the ninth plague, three days of darkness, as the result of the severe *hamsin* wind that blows from the Sahara, carrying with it sand and dust. In that particular year, the cumulatively devastating effects of the previous plagues on the soil caused the matter released into the atmosphere to be extraordinarily dense and abundant, blocking out the sun. Since the Israelites were largely domiciled on the higher ground of Goshen, they were not affected.

Consider the perception of the parties concerned. The Egyptians, Pharaoh included, would have seen the plague of darkness as a humiliation of the sun god Amon-Re—a crushing blow. The sun was regarded as the first king of Egypt from whom the pharaohs descended.

It was through the ingenuity of Moses that the Israelites, who resided on higher ground, were not engulfed in darkness. They would have regarded the darkness as the will of their God inflicted selectively on the Egyptians. Hört also speculated that the Israelites would not have felt the impacts of the plagues of insects, pestilence, and boils as selective punishment, as well. Now it can be seen why God was said to stiffen Pharaoh's heart so all could witness His presence and supremacy.

The strong probability that the plagues were natural occurrences caused by abnormal inundations of the river does not diminish their perception as manifestations of God's glory. He apparently employed forces of nature to negate the relevance of Egyptian deities and magicians to convince Pharaoh to free the slaves.

The tenth plague, death of the first born, was another story; Hört didn't deal with it. Unlike the fist nine, it does not appear to be an act of nature. My grandfather who chose to skip the plagues in the Passover seder might have thought otherwise about the first nine if he had known about Greta Hört. The tenth would have remained an enigma to him. However, it too has some justification.

> Moses said, "Thus says the Lord: 'Toward midnight I will go forth among the Egyptians, and every first born in the land of Egypt shall die, from the first born of Pharaoh who sits on the throne to the first born of the slave girl... but not a dog shall snarl at any of the Israelites, at man or beast—in order that you may know that the Lord makes a distinction between Egypt and Israel.'"
>
> Exodus 11:4–7

The tenth plague resonates with the sound of retribution for Pharaoh's father charging his people, "Every boy that is born you shall throw into the Nile" (Exodus 1:22).

If payback comes to mind, we would do well to consider another possibility; Pharaoh's first son died at about the same time. A hieroglyphic inscription, discovered in a tomb in the Valley of the Kings, bears the name of Ramses' first born. His death is estimated to have occurred between 1259 and 1248, about the time of the Exodus and might have been related to the plagues. Ascribing cause and effect relationships to comparable events is quite common.

According to Fredrichs and Lesko in their study, *Exodus, the Egyptian Evidence*, the idea of the death of the firstborn corresponds to papyrus, "Admonitions": "Indeed men are few, and he who places his brother in the ground is everywhere. Indeed hearts are violent, pestilence is throughout the land, blood is everywhere, death is not lacking, and the mummy-cloth speaks even before one comes near it."[4]

Gary Greenberg, in *Myths of the Bible*, opines, "From a literary standpoint, the Bible and the Admonitions each described Egypt under similar circumstances in different time frames... there was nothing miraculous about the conditions described, nor do we have any evidence from Egyptian records that the firstborn child of every Egyptian family died on one night. Such an event would not have gone unnoticed."[5]

My grandfather would probably have accepted the explanation of the fist nine plagues as natural occurrences. If he had also known about Ramses' son, the tenth might have been included as having validity.

The level of optimism was so high among the Israelites that, even before smiting the first born, negotiations appeared to be going favorably and deliverance would soon occur.

The celebration began immediately.

"The Lord said to Moses and Aaron in the land of Egypt: This month shall mark for you the beginning of the months: it shall be the first of the months of the year for you" (Exodus 12:1–2).

The Israelites were directed to paint the lintels of their houses with lamb's blood and stay home. Thus, when in the middle of the night the Lord struck down the first born of the Egyptians, he would know to pass over the houses of the Israelites.

"And Pharaoh summoned Moses and Aaron in the night and said, 'Up, depart from among my people, you and the Israelites with you! Go, worship the Lord as you said!'" (Exodus 12:31).

The show was over. At this point in the historical drama, it might seem that the Passover was anticlimactic. From hindsight it probably was. But consider yourself as being there, a slave who had just been liberated from a lifetime of bondage. You would never have to bake another brick beneath the Egyptian rod.

Until now, you would have experienced inhuman coercion exerted by a despot and been taught to revere omnipotent and fearsome Egyptian deities. Now, all has changed. The beneficent God, as Moses and Aaron promised, had subjugated Pharaoh and subordinated his deities. For the first time ever, you made an existential choice that created a feeling of identity.

It follows that God told Moses to forge into the Israelites' memory experiences of the wonder of an invisible God—a God committed to lead them from the land of desperation to one flowing with milk and honey. They were never to forget, and they were to reinforce the message on their children that they were once slaves in Egypt.

> And you shall explain to your son on that day, "It is because of what the Lord did for me when I went free from Egypt. And this shall serve you as a sign on your hand and as a reminder on your forehead."
>
> Exodus 13:8–9

As I write this, we are dedicating a week commemorating the anniversary of the liberation of Auschwitz—another ignominious period of history the world must never forget. We have museums, galleries, movies, and religious services to emblazon the memory in our collective conscious. The lessons of history must never be forgotten.

Just before the final curtain, Moses enunciated an existential motif of memory destined to transform a rabble into a people: "Remember this day, on which you went free from Egypt, the house of bondage, How the Lord freed you from it with a mighty hand" (13:3).

RADICAL AMAZEMENT

> The length of time that the Israelites lived in Egypt was four hundred and thirty years; at the end of the four hundred and thirtieth year, to the very day, all the ranks of the Lord departed from the land of Egypt.
>
> Exodus 12:40–41

From Price, Sellers, and Carlson we gain insight from an Egyptian standpoint from their study, *The Monuments and the Old Testament*: "Important as this day was for the Israelites, it was no watershed in Egyptian history. We know of it only from the Bible. Egyptian scribes tell us nothing of such an escape. It is not likely they would have felt any need to record it. Such migrations occurred frequently in lands of shepherds and nomads."[1]

Had the Israelites numbered a million, or even hundreds of thousands, the Egyptian scribes most certainly would have noticed. Similarly, had all the first born of Egypt died, it would have been recorded. The impact on civilization was yet to be determined.

Will Durant's *Our Oriental Heritage* describes the onset of their departure: "In preference to going directly to Sinai, they took a circuitous route to avoid belligerent desert tribes. The route was one laid down by Egyptian turquoise hunting expeditions one thousand years earlier, which probably was familiar to Moses."[2]

"The Lord went before them in a pillar of cloud by day, to guide them along the way, and in a pillar of fire by night that they might travel by day and night" (13:21).

From Nahum Sarna's *Exploring Exodus*, we get the following explanation, "The pillars of smoke and fire express the idea of the Divine Presence extending unfailing guidance and protection, here and throughout the wanderings."[3] They proceeded until they formed an encampment facing the Sea of Reeds.

When the King of Egypt heard the people had fled, he took off in rapid pursuit with officers and more than six hundred chariots. Apparently, an event that was not important to the Egyptian scribes elicited the king's personal attention.

> As Pharaoh drew near, the Israelites caught sight of the Egyptians advancing upon them. Greatly frightened, the Israelites cried out to the Lord. And said to Moses, "Was it for want of graves in Egypt that you brought us to die in the wilderness?" But Moses said to the people, "Have no fear! Stand by, and witness the deliverance the Lord will work for you today; The Egyptians whom you see today you will never see again."
>
> Exodus 13:10–13

There is an appropriate *midrash* that cries out to be inserted at this point. It is so compelling with its human and universal message that the Bible does not seem complete without it. Rabbi Norman Cohen gave it the title "The Leap of Nachshon ben Amminadab."

> When the Israelites stood at the sea and the angry, turbulent waters confronted them, this tribe said, "I will not enter the water first." And another tribe said, "I will not be the first." And so said others. While they were standing there arguing, Nachshon jumped up and went down into the sea, falling into the waves he began to flounder in the water.
>
> Of him, it is said, "Save me, O God, for the waters are come over my soul… I am come into deep waters, and the flood overwhelms me."
>
> (Psalm 69:2–3)

We can now understand why Moses cried out to God as the Israelites stood on the shore. Seeing the water about to swallow Nachshon and aware of the Egyptians approaching, Moses prayed to God to intervene on Nachshon's behalf. God, however, chastised Moses for thinking that prayer alone would be efficacious and urged him to do something to save his friend and the people.

The existential implication was clearly that God had given Moses a mind, a rod, and freedom of choice. He was empowered to make the decision of what to do. And so Moses lifted up his rod, the sea parted, and the Israelites crossed on dry land. In context, God might have said, "I freed the Hebrews so they could make free choices, and that includes you."

After the Israelites had crossed on dry land, Moses held up his arm, and the sea closed on the Egyptians, their chariots, and their horsemen. When I was young, I could never understand why God let the horses drown. They had done nothing to warrant such inhumane punishment.

The Nachshon *midrash* exemplifies why some are uncomfortable with existentialism. They see its central principle as individuals being condemned to freedom—having to make choices. Even Moses when confronted with a difficult decision sought to avoid making a choice by imploring God for help.

Sartre said that existentialists carry the whole weight of the world on their shoulders because they are responsible for the world and themselves in it. For some, it's onerous to decide where to go for dinner.

Let's think about what happened. In the Bible, it's portrayed dramatically.

> Moses held out his arm over the sea and the Lord drove back the sea with a strong east wind... the waters forming a wall for them on their right and on their left... And when Israel saw the wondrous power which the Lord had wielded against the Egyptians, the people feared the Lord; they had faith in the Lord and His servant Moses.
>
> 14:21–23

Were the laws of nature negated? A more appropriate question is did the people witness a miracle? In Heschel's words, "A miracle is not an act interfering with the normal course of natural events, but an act creating the perception of an exceptional moment—a moment of radical amazement."

We know the narrator of Exodus was capable of dramatic flair. The exaggerated numbers of Israelites and Egyptians who participated are irrelevant. However, walls of water, standing on either side, forming a passage of dry land might make great theater, but in the wilderness—as everywhere else—water is known to seek its own level.

The drowning of Pharaoh's army may have been drawn from an Egyptian story told in the Book of the Divine Cow about a time when humanity revolted against the rule of the god Re. The myth tells of a Reed Marsh where the enemies of Re lay slaughtered and the fields flooded over with a red liquid.[4]

Consider a logical explanation of what might have happened at the sea. It's possible that during his military training, Moses visited the Sea of Reeds area. He may also have roamed there during his sojourn in the wilderness.

In either case, his knowledge of the territory would have enabled him to lead the people to a place where they could walk across the Sea of Reeds, but horses and chariots would get stuck in the muck. In the Torah, it's expressed more dramatically: "[God] locked the wheels of their chariots so that they moved forward with difficulty" (Exodus 14:25).

Here's a question for anyone who has seen the 1956 movie *The Ten Commandments*. What is the first recollection from the movie that comes to mind? Even if asked out of context, most would respond with the crossing of the sea. Cecil B. De-Mille created on film the scene as described in the Bible.

Moses raised his rod; the waters separated, creating huge walls of water frozen in time. Thousands of people in desert dress rushed across to the other shore pursued by Egyptians in horse drawn chariots. At the moment the last Israelite reached the far shore, Moses held out his arm, and the waters engulfed the Egyptian troops.

Had the scene occurred according to my conjecture of what might have happened, it would have been discarded on the cutting room floor. Thanks to the narrator's poetic license, the story, preserved in the art form of metaphor, has been told by mothers and fathers to their sons and daughter as if they themselves had been there when God parted the sea. Any less dramatic conjecture would not likely have elicited much attention.

What would we have done had we been there? What would we have thought if after years beneath the yolk of Egyptian oppression, we had avoided imminent death from the swords of the pursuers?

We would have looked back at the scene of the enemy struggling to survive the inundation of water and been dazed in wonder and gratitude. From where there had been no hope there was now a vision of the future.

Moses had prayed to an invisible God to whom he attributed the miraculous events that liberated us from our oppressors. But because we could not see this invisible God and we could see Moses, from our perspective, Moses had been our savior. It was obviously Moses who had the audacity to confront the mighty king. We had just seen how Moses led us across the sea and then drowned the Egyptians in it.

We had been taught Egyptian deities could be seen and heard; Moses was more like them than the God he spoke of.

Moses sensed this adoration and reversion to idolatry of the rabble in his care. This was not intended to be an ego trip for him. He knew he must integrate the ecstasy of rescue with the perception that it was God who had saved them.

To make his point, what better means of emotional expression than in song—a song of rejoicing and thanksgiving glorifying the Lord. He gathered the people together and they sang:

> I will sing this song to the Lord, for He has triumphed gloriously; Horse and driver He has hurled into the sea. The Lord is my strength and might; He is become my deliverance. This is my God and I will enshrine Him; The God of my father, and I will exalt Him. The Lord, the Warrior—YHVH is His name…. Who is like You, O Lord among the celestials; Who is like You, majestic in Holiness, Awesome in splendor, working wonders!… The Lord will reign forever and ever!
>
> Exodus 15:1–3, 11, 18

A question is usually an interrogative sentence calling for a positive or negative answer. "But the sentence,

'*Who is like You?*'" Heschel explains, "is a question that contains the impossibility of giving a negative answer; it is an answer in disguise; a question of amazement not of curiosity."[5]

The song is familiar. I've sung it hundreds of times. The poem is so moving, and the drama so intense that simply the act of typing the words becomes a mystical experience. Little wonder that some interpreters have said the Israelites actually saw God at the sea as they sang this song. It transformed their experiences related to liberation into a perception of radical amazement.

Because of its length, I have provided only fragments of the song; the source is indicated. Of particular interest is the appearance of the idea of *Holiness* for the third time in Exodus. Derived from the designation of separation of time or space, it is no longer limited to that denotation. Moses expanded its meaning to define the ideal manifestation of God—a true stroke of genius.

It becomes increasingly apparent that, much as Moses wanted his flock to comprehend God, above all, he wanted them to feel God's presence—to emotionally experience God. He sought to awaken the idea of God's Holiness conveying rapture and exaltation. Ultimately, to achieve, in Rudolph Otto's words, "the feeling of the uncanny, the thrill of reverence, the sense of dependence."[6]

Scholars such as Philo and others believe the song was sung antiphonally. That is, Moses taught the people the chorus, which they would repeat after each verse which Moses sang. Of course, there is no record of the melody, but there is a contemporary setting, composed by Jacob Weinberg, that I sang antiphonally with the religious school choirs of Temple Beth El. The words were paraphrased to fit the music:

Sound the Loud Timbrel[d]

Chorus
Sound the loud timbrel o'er Egypt's dark sea!
The Lord hath triumphed, His people are free!
Sound the loud tumbrel, o'er Egypt's dark sea!
The Lord hath triumphed, His people are free!

Solo
Sing for the pride of the tyrant is broken,
His chariots, his horsemen
all splendid and brave,
How vain was their boasting,
the Lord hath but spoken,
And chariots and horsemen
are sunk in the wave.

The chorus is repeated several times and, each time, followed by a different verse. The song concludes with the congregation joining in the final chorus.

I continue to meet adults I haven't seen since they were in religious school who remember singing the song at the sea. They seldom recall the name, but they haven't forgotten the mystical experience. Great is the power of song and the gratification of singing it with children.

---

[d] Timbrel: An ancient percussion instrument similar to a tambourine.

It has been said the rejoicing continued until late that night. Moses' entire family got into the act: Miriam, the sister of Moses and Aaron, took timbrel in hand and led the women in dance and song.

And so we teach it to our children—the history entwined with metaphor. We retell the story in the words of the narrator—conscious of its anachronisms and exaggerations—because it works. We are able to recreate the reality of the existential experience through metaphor.

Cynthia Ozick, one of the most cogent writers in the current literary scene, expressed it eloquently in her collection of essays, "Metaphor and Memory." "Four hundred years of bondage in Egypt, rendered as metaphoric memory can be spoken in a moment; in a single sentence: 'Because *you* were strangers in the land of Egypt.'"[7]

I think Ozick summed it up better than I could.

Another aspect of radical amazement we have witnessed is the mind's ability to create metaphors.

> When Israel went forth from Egypt... The sea saw them and fled, Jordan ran backward, Mountains skipped like rams. Hills like sheep.
>
> Psalm 114:3-4

THE PARTY'S OVER

When the celebration of singing and dancing ended, Moses and the Israelites began the journey to Sinai. No water was found until after three days travel they arrived at Marah, but the water was too bitter to drink.

"And the people grumbled against Moses saying, 'What shall we drink?'" (Exodus 15:24). The Lord showed Moses a piece of wood, which Moses threw into the water and the water became sweet.

The relevance of water is cogently expressed by Mary Ellen Chase: "Water itself forms countless images, more indeed than any other miracle of God's creation except mountains and hills, for in this parched and thirsty land it meant life and hope."[1]

God then made a *fixed rule* that if they would heed Him and do what was right in His sight, He would not cause them to suffer the diseases He brought on the Egyptians. By the severe trial of the lack of water, He taught them that the Lord would *be their healer* if only they remained loyal to His precepts. Umberto Cassuto observed in *A Commentary on the Book of Exodus*, "As I have now healed the water, so

I will protect you from all sickness."[2] Divine healing follows divine law.

After one month and fifteen days, "the whole Israelite community grumbled against Moses and Aaron. 'If only we had died by the hand of the Lord in the land of Egypt, when we sat by the fleshpots, when we ate our fill of bread! For you have brought us into the wilderness to starve'" (Exodus 16:3).

Moses and Aaron explained to the people that their grumbling was against God and not against them, and this was God's response to Moses: "I have heard the grumblings of the Israelites. Speak to them and say: By evening you shall eat flesh, and in the morning you shall have your fill of bread; and you shall know that I the Lord am your God" (Exodus 16:11).

Each day for five days, they received and gathered just the right amount of flesh and bread (quail and manna) to satisfy everyone. On the sixth day, they got double the amount to suffice for the seventh day on which they would not have to gather food. The seventh day was to be a day of rest provided by the Lord.

They advanced by stages until they encamped at Rephidim where there was, again, no water to drink. They quarreled, grumbled at Moses, and asked, "Why did you bring us up from Egypt, to kill us and our children and our livestock from thirst?" (Exodus 17:3).

Moses sought help from the Lord who told him to strike the rock at Horeb with his rod, and water would issue from it, another act that would produce the appearance of radical amazement.

The place was named Massah and Meribah, because the Israelites quarreled and because they tried the Lord, saying, "Is the Lord present among us or not?

Exodus 17:7

Moses was beginning to comprehend the magnitude of dealing with a pitiful rabble of humanity with no sense of appreciation and, like the petulant mother-in-law paradigm, full of complaints. He was also getting a lesson in group dynamics—the restiveness of the behavior of a crowd. Individually, his followers might have been reasonable, but as a cohesive group, their grumbling became endemic.

Buber proposes that "only now, in the hour of disillusion at finding the people not yet truly a people, and certainly not a people of *YHVH*, only now does the thought come to Moses of the covenant which shall simultaneously unite the tribes into a people and bind the people to their God."[3]

The moment was one of luminosity for Moses. The party was over, leaving a monumental challenge, perhaps one not fully anticipated.

The mumbling and grumbling exposed the need for a sense of belonging, the need for each family to identify as belonging to an organization. At least in Egypt, they had belonged to a society of slaves even though there was no pride in membership.

But the worst was yet to come. While camped at Rephidim, the tribe of Amalek launched a surprise attack on them. Moses chose Joshua[e] to select a force of men to go forth and do battle.

They actually succeeded in a strange way. Moses positioned himself atop a hill with the rod of God in his hand. When he raised his arms, Israel prevailed; but when he lowered his arms, the Amalekites seized the advantage. However, Aaron and Hur[f] interceded and held Moses' arms extended until sunset. "Joshua overwhelmed the people of Amalek with his sword" (Exodus 17:13).

A rabbinic comment on Moses' uplifted arms during the course of the battle suggests Divine intervention. The Lord was so incensed by the ruthlessness of the attack that he declared to Moses, "I will utterly blot out the memory of Amalek from under heaven" (Exodus 17:14). A reminder of the encounter is found in Deuteronomy:

> Remember what Amalek did to you on your journey, after you left Egypt—how, undeterred by fear of God, he surprised you on the march when you were famished and weary, and cut down all the stragglers in your rear.
>
> Deuteronomy 25:17-19

Originally, I intended to leap from the Sea of Reeds to Sinai, omitting Exodus chapters 16 and 17. The

---

[e] Joshua was Moses' faithful attendant and became his designated successor.

[f] Hur, like Joshua, must have been an important public figure and was later associated with Aaron.

ugliness of murmuring and grumbling is not appealing at this point (there's even more of it later). However, thinking about the rock created two issues I could not leave out.

As a child in religious school, I was awestruck by the miracle of God having Moses whack a rock so hard that enough water came out to satisfy all those people. No one ever told me miracles are in the eye of the beholder. The same was true for the Israelites.

The further relevance of the rock is referred to in rabbinic explanations of repetition in the Bible. Reiteration of words and events was the writers' way of recording events of extreme importance—there is no needless duplication in the Bible.

It was so with the case of the rock. The incident was told again in Numbers 20:11 in similar fashion when the thirsty Israelites were camped at Kadesh on their way to the Promised Land. The second occurrence inspired the legend that the rock containing water followed Israel through the desert for forty years.

Much would have been lost if we had not followed the trek across the sand from the sea to the mountain. Besides missing the rock, we would not have known about the sweetening of bitter water, the quails in the evening, the manna each morning, and the idea of rest on the seventh day in anticipation of the commandment.

The battle with the Amalekites might be the most important loss of all. While war is hardly to be glorified, victory over an aggressor would have created a unifying bond among the people. If winning a Super Bowl can amalgamate a community, imagine what a military victory did for a downtrodden rabble.

The messages to be taken from this part of the journey are the touch points of perception reinforced by the self-effacing Moses; the people were to be witness to God's intervention.

Was it part of Moses' grand plan? He had lived in the desert for more than fifty years and experienced innumerable hardships. He certainly knew where to find food and water. It seems that he could have prepared a disaster plan to make the trip more endurable than as experienced.

But had Moses made it look easy and had no hardships been endured, the appearance of Divine intervention would not have been called for. It was only as a result of the deprivations that they encountered that the alleviation of suffering could be witness to God's intervention. We have learned to call it radical amazement. Moses' concern was to reinforce the perception that God had interceded. He capitalized on the hardships that he knew would be encountered to create that existential perception.

It was probably true that the life of wanderers in the desert was in many ways more difficult than life as slaves in Egypt. Freedom from taskmasters did not produce total escape from misery and anxiety. They were now homeless, without sufficient food and water, and separated from the familiar Egyptian deities that gave them a degree of comfort.

Their wandering bears a striking congruence to the original adherents of existentialism who were mostly central Europeans caught in the crevice between two world wars. They too were subject to a triple alienation: loss of God whom Nietzsche had declared dead, rampant inflation, and an inhospitable social and political climate.

This later triple alienation presents an interesting comparison to the Exodus from Egypt with one striking difference; in Europe there was no Moses.

> Like a hart crying for water, My soul cries for
> You, O God;
> My soul thirsts for God, the living God.
>
> Psalm 42:1-2

A MATTER OF CHOICE

> On the third new moon after the Israelites
> had gone forth from the land of Egypt… they
> entered the wilderness of Sinai… and encamped
> there in front of the mountain, and Moses went
> up to God.
>
> Exodus 9:1–2

Seven weeks after the Israelites left Egypt, they encamped at the foot of a cloud-covered mountain in the barren wilderness of Sinai. We have been told of the troubles they endured during the journey—thirst, hunger, and the Amalekites, but what else? Having driven across a stretch of that desert with Shalom in search of the mountain, I would have expected much worse—serpents, insects, animals, disease, sandstorms and all sorts of other discomforts. Perhaps the writer thought he had made his point.

Moses did his best to provide aid and then tell the Israelites that God assisted. He used the vagaries of nature in an ingenious way to endow God with properties and qualities the people could grasp. The net effect was to prepare them for the ensuing encounter when God would give with one hand and seek commitment with the other.

> The Lord called to [Moses] from the mountain, saying, "Thus shall you say to the house of Jacob and declare to the children of Israel: 'You have seen what I did to the Egyptians, how I bore you on eagles' wings and brought you to Me. Now, then, if you will obey Me faithfully and keep My commandments, you shall be My treasured possession among all the peoples. Indeed all the earth is Mine, but you shall be to Me a kingdom of priests and a Holy nation.' These are the words that you shall speak to the children of Israel."
>
> Exodus 19:3–6

In the above and the verses that follow, Moses went up and down the mountain many times to hear the words God wanted delivered to the people. The text is convoluted and confusing, but this much is clear—God spoke only to Moses who, in turn, conveyed his words to the people.

One can but envy Chaim Potok's gift of poetic expression in paraphrasing the text:

> A cloud obscures the mountain; words obscure the event. The narrative of the Revelation on Mount Sinai is a labyrinth of dark passages that wind through abrupt turns and lurch across sudden chasms... The Bible seems helpless before the event, at a loss how to shape it with words.[1]

God reminded the people of how He punished Pharaoh and the Egyptians on their behalf. There follows the elegant metaphor in which God compares Himself to the eagle, the king of birds. The eagle, an Egyptian symbol familiar to the Israelites, was capable of soaring to great heights carrying its young on its back.

Nehama Leibowitz, in her *Studies in Shemot (Exodus)*, explains, "His role, as your Lord, consists of bringing out this intervention in your life, this direction given you, this leading you from Egypt to this point."[2] *And brought you to Me.* Where was that? A place where they had been taught deities reside—a place the Israelites could relate to—the top of a mountain.

Now, the Israelites were challenged with making an existential choice. God presented the proposal that *if you will obey Me faithfully and keep my commandments, you shall be My treasured possession.* It was up to the Israelites. For the first time, they experienced the responsibility of choice concomitant with freedom. By choosing to keep God's commandments, they would become his treasured possession.

To us, three thousand years later, it sounds like an obvious decision since the alternative was to return to Egypt and carry on as before. But from the people's perspective, it was not that simple.

While Egypt meant endless toil in the hot sun, it also meant the assurance of enough to eat and drink. There the greatest choice that would confront them would be how to avoid the taskmaster's lash. They could return to a situation that was known and life would be simple. They knew what awaited them in Egypt.

On the other hand, God's proposal was replete with ambiguities. They must have questioned what God meant by "My commandments." What would the land of milk and honey be like? Their ingrained fear of authority prompted them to question an unknown source of power. After all, Pharaoh too was understood to be a god.

The sure thing was certainly not attractive, but the unknown alternative might have even more serious shortcomings. It had been rewarding to watch the Egyptians floundering in the sea, but trudging across the desert was not going to be like walking along the banks of the Nile.

Sartre's writings are filled with many such uncertain choices demanding decisions that could redirect the actuality of one's own life and those of others. An example is a compelling anecdote, that of a young man who had assumed the care of his ailing mother whom he dearly loved. When he received a call from the French army to serve a tour of duty, he had to choose between his helpless mother and his beloved country.

Sartre insisted that each person's freedom of choice impacted all humankind. At Sinai, the men had to choose on behalf of themselves, their families, and the community. Although, beyond their comprehension, in their act of choice was not merely "This is what I choose," but also "This is what is to be chosen." Without knowing it, they were determining what all mankind everywhere was forever to become.[3]

Rabbi Richard L. Rubenstein summed it up in his perception: "There is virtually no idea that is stressed more in the Bible than human freedom of choice."[4]

The final component of God's offer was "you shall be a kingdom of priests and a Holy nation." Buber interprets *kingdom of priests* as meaning a "royal retinue" around the king. To take it one step further, it suggests acting as priests by doing God's will through ministering and caring for others.

From the Torah commentaries of Rabbi W. Gunther Plaut, we read, "One may assume the 'royal retinue' would have been seen by the people as a familiar setting—the divine Sovereign covenanting with those He promised to protect."[5] This is the dichotomy of ideas we will find recurring in the text. Moses tried to create a separation between past and future, life under Pharaoh and life with God. At the same time, he endeavored to retain an existential link with familiar Egyptian religious practices.

In the present context of *a Holy nation,* Holiness continues to take on new dimensions. Conjoined with *a kingdom of priests,* it arouses elevated feelings of duty, honor, and loyalty. Considering the origin of the term, we should understand it to establish a separation, a unique identity apart from the Egyptians.

The idea of "you shall be My treasured possession" took on the context of the Israelites' becoming God's "chosen people" as a survival mechanism that lead to the longevity of the Jewish people. In the present context, the meaning appears to be clearly one of an offer and an unconditional acceptance.

The idea of special election ignored the fact that they were not a homogeneous people. In Exodus 12:38, those who left Egypt were spoken of as a *mixed multitude*, implying the inclusion of slaves other than descendants of Abraham. We find further confirmation in Numbers 11:4 *the riffraff in their midst.*

In presenting God's words, Moses was able to refocus the people's vision on the half-full glass, not the half-empty one. They forgot that their throats were once parched with thirst and remembered that God gave them water. They put aside their recollection of hunger pangs and recalled it was the Lord who gave them bread and meat. The relevance of desert hardships became dwarfed by the radical amazement of God's grace. When Moses conveyed this message to the people, "All the people answered as one, saying, 'All that the Lord has spoken we will do!' And Moses brought back the people's words to the Lord" (Exodus 9:8).

From Heschel' treatise, *Man is not Alone*: "The endless distance between God and the human mind was pierced, and man was told that God is concerned with the affairs of man; that not only does man need God, God also is in need of man. It is such knowledge that makes the soul of man immune to despair."[6]

> How odd of God to choose the Jews. But what's more odd, the Jews chose God.
>
> —Hertz[7]

THE TEN UTTERANCES

The stage is now set for the one of the greatest moments in the history of humankind—the central and most exalted theme of the Grand Narrative.

God came down to the mountain, which had been enshrouded in a thick cloud. Moses then ascended the mountain to speak to God who gave him messages to deliver to the people. There ensued a recurring pattern of Moses climbing up the mountain and returning with messages.

The mountain is understood to be the same mountain, Mount Horeb, where Moses encountered God in the burning bush. It, henceforth, will be called Mount Sinai.[1]

A perception was created of bridging the gap between heaven and earth. The invisible God was validating his authenticity—as a deity should—by maintaining an obscure abode atop a mountain.

Clearly, the people had no knowledge of what was going on up there other than what Moses related. There were no witnesses because their vision was obscured by cloud cover and they could hear no voices.

To assure obscurity, one of God's messages was the prohibition, "You shall set bounds for the people round about, saying, 'Beware of going up the mountain or touching the border of it. Whoever touches the border of it shall be put to death'" (Exodus 19:12).

The following is Potok's eloquently moving condensation of the text:

> On the third day the mountain, covered in boiling smoke, trembles violently. The horns blare louder and louder. Moses speaks. God responds in thunder and comes down to the mountain. God calls to Moses from the top of the mountain. Moses goes up to him. God tells Moses to go down and warn the people not to "break through to the Lord to gaze, lest many of them perish." Moses tells God that the people cannot come up to Mount Sinai, "for you warned me, saying, 'Set bounds upon the mountain and sanctify it.'" God then orders Moses to bring Aaron up the mountain, but we are told nothing more of this.[2]

"And Moses went down to the people and spoke to them" (Exodus 19:25).

God spoke all these words, saying: "I the Lord am your God who brought you out of the land of Egypt, the house of bondage" (Exodus 20:1).

These words, which begin at Exodus 20:1 are the first of the Ten Utterances. They follow directly after Exodus 19:25 with no elision to bridge the gap between what Moses said and the words of God. One would expect a dramatic prolonged silence after the noise and tumult, presumably of natural causes, announcing the appearance of YHVH, but the text conveyed no apparent silence.

Pauses for dramatic effect are essential in artistic performances, such as music and drama. I recall attending a piano workshop in Ann Arbor, taught by the eminent Artur Schnabel who is famous for his interpretations of Beethoven, Brahms, and Schubert. In his comments to student pianists, he had two things to say about silence in music.

With respect to interpretation, "It is a given that an accomplished pianist will play the notes correctly. The attention to the spaces between the notes is the hall-mark of the artist." And with respect to performance: "After a forte climax in the orchestra, the pianist must wait for the reverberation in the hall to subside before proceeding."

Would not the Ultimate Artist have provided a moment of existential silence after the tumultuous fanfare so each could experience the reverberations in their own way? We have spoken about the need to fill in gaps in the text. In this case, we miss the existence of one.

A gap does occur later in the Bible, in 1 Kings 19:11–12. When the Lord appeared before Elijah, there was a great wind, an earthquake, and fire, but the Lord was not in any of them. *And after the fire—a thin quiet voice.*

Having been introduced to the staging, let us proceed to discover the existential components of the first utterance. Professor Mortimer J. Adler who taught the *Great Books Course* at the University of Chicago would frequently introduce a difficult concept with the suggestion, "Let us think this through together."

I. I, YHVH, am your God who brought you out of the land of Egypt, the house of bondage.

It is useful to think of what God might have said and didn't. God did not say, "I am the Lord, the source of all being." That would have been too abstract for the people to comprehend. God did not say, "I am the Lord who created the world and all its inhabitants." This might have been better, but it would have been related to biblical history of which the people had no knowledge.

What God did say was, "I am the Lord who brought you out of the land of Egypt." This was a reminder that he had performed "acts of radical amazement" to liberate the Israelites so that he might be their God. This was a fitting declaration intended to lead to an acceptance of the utterances that were to follow.

The difficulty of actually apprehending God is neatly captured by Rabbi Yochanan who suggested in the second century that each and every person at Sinai experienced the Revelation differently, "each according to what he or she could bear."[3]

A subtle existential implication, not apparent in the English translation, can be found in rabbinic literature. "Suddenly they heard the Divine Voice utter the opening word, *Anochi,* 'It is I.' God employed the Egyptian *Anochi* instead of the Hebrew word *Ani,* because even as a mortal king would welcome his son upon his return after a lengthy stay in a distant land by addressing him in the language of that country, so did the Lord speak to them in the familiar Egyptian term in order that they cease trembling and feel reassured."[4]

The first letter in the Hebrew word *anochi* is *aleph*, which is a silent letter, not vocalized. The mystics attribute only the aleph as spoken by God, perhaps subtly representing that additional moment of silence enhancing the preceding stillness.

By using the prism, we are beginning to discover hidden existential meanings in the Grand Narrative.

II. You shall have no other gods before me. You shall not make for yourself a sculptured image, or any likeness of what is in the heavens above, or on the earth below, or in the waters under the earth. You shall not bow down to them or serve them. For I the Lord your God am an impassioned God, visiting the guilt of the parents upon the children, upon the third and upon the fourth generations of those who reject me, but showing steadfast love (*chesed*) to the thousandth generation of those who love me and keep my commandments.

III. You shall not swear falsely by the name of the Lord your God; for the Lord will not clear one who swears falsely by his name.

Utterances II and III should be discussed together because of their conjoined nature. They set forth what must be the relationship of the Israelites to the Lord: God's presence was not to be confused with a visual or material representation. The worship of other deities was rigorously forbidden.

Together, they represent the most difficult of God's injunctions for the Israelites to observe because they ordained virtually severing their umbilical cords with the past. On prior occasions, Moses had tried to create links with Egyptian experiences to help the people connect with the invisible God; now a severe disconnect was inevitable.

They must break new ground in their relationship with God, transcending all preceding experience of the worship of pagan deities. The idea of the immanence of God was to supplant the idol worship prevalent in Egypt.

Although the second utterance is crafted in a negative sense, Isaac Arama finds in it a liberating, positive dynamic quality: besides a warning that prohibits the worship of any other deity, the utterance breathes a wonderful message of freedom, that since He is our God, and near to us, what need have we to obey any other lordship.

The choice of words deserves a closer look. Lost in translation is the Hebrew stylistic aspects that *you* in the utterances, numbers 2-4 and 6-10 is in all cases implied as singular. The English equivalent is vague in this regard; the English *you* can be either singular or plural. Lacking the specificity of the Hebrew intention—a regrettable ambiguity of the English language; the utterances were directed to each individual, not to the people collectively.

In chapter three, "Where Sinai Is Today," we discussed a cardinal principle of existentialism, the responsibility of the individual to determine what he or she will become. By addressing the utterances to each individual, *you*, in the midst of the multitude emphasized the existential accountability of individual freedom of choice woven throughout the biblical tapestry.

The first part of the second utterance reflects the legal style in a treaty between a Hittite king and Egypt with a startling innovation. After stating the punishment of visiting the guilt of the parents who reject him upon their children, God tendered the reward of steadfast love for keeping his commandments—a choice that makes it more compelling.

> IV. Remember the Sabbath day and keep it Holy. Six days you shall labor and do all your work, but the seventh day is a Sabbath of the Lord your God: you shall not do any work—you, your son, your male or female slave, or your cattle, or the stranger who is within your settlements. For in six days the Lord made heaven and earth and sea, and all that is in them, and He rested on the seventh day; therefore the Lord blessed the Sabbath day and hallowed it.

The second and third utterances commanded such a severe change in the attitudes of those assembled that some compensation for the loss of images was in order. This reward took the form of a weekly day of rest—something beyond the wildest expectations of the people. The creation of the Sabbath compensated for the elimination of objects of worship many times over. As further enhancement of the idea of freedom, even slaves and cattle were included—a largesse that must have sounded a positive note.

We need to note in particular the first word, *remember*. Not only were the people enjoined not to forget to rest on the seventh day, but to remember when there was no Sabbath. In contrast, when the utterance is repeated in Deuteronomy 5, the verb *observe* replaces *remember*. By that time, the commandment was directed to a subsequent generation, a generation that had not known the absence of a Sabbath.

In the first utterance, God was introduced as the liberator, expressing concern for those who suffered under Pharaoh's yoke. Now, the people are told of God as the creator of heaven and earth—relating it to the process of creation in Genesis as having taken place over six days following which God rested. "And God blessed the seventh day and declared it Holy" (Genesis 2:3). It was a loving gift of God to share the Holiness of a day of rest with those of his creation.

In the ten utterances, the term *Holy* is applied to one utterance only, the Sabbath. Indeed, the idea of Holy as separation of time connotes the holiness of time. We have discussed before Moses' objective to associate the idea of Holy with experiencing the presence of God. Here that idea is further developed.

According to Heschel, "The law of the Sabbath tries to direct the body and the mind to the dimension of the Holy."[5] If we fast forward to Exodus 31:13–14 we read:

> You must keep My Sabbaths, for this is a sign
> between Me and you throughout the ages, that
> you may know that I the Lord have consecrated
> you. You shall keep the Sabbath, for it is Holy
> for you.

It helps to understand that the biblical phrase "a sign between Me and you" was also used to express the relation between bride and bridegroom. In this sense, it is used as a metaphor symbolizing the intimate bond between God and humankind. The Sabbath is the bride and the celebration of the Sabbath, a wedding.

Returning to Exodus 20:12:

V. Honor your father and your mother that you may long endure on the land that the Lord your God is assigning to you.

Does the gravity of honoring parents approach that of the preceding four? The answer is found in the first Hebrew word, *kavod*, in this sense translated as "honor," but also meaning "glorify" and "revere." In terms of creating an orderly society, honoring parents is indeed near the top of the list.

For one thing, Moses must have been disturbed by the Egyptian infatuation with an afterlife. Conversely, Moses was more concerned with the matter of living than that of dying. The people had lived with the pyramids, statuary, and ceremonies ennobling life in the hereafter. They were aware of priests accepting payments from the wealthy, no matter how insidious their lives, to assure successful passage beyond the tomb.

Moses was convinced Egyptian funerary rites were an abomination, but what was to be offered in their place? For the Israelites to be honored and remembered by their children. Their children, in turn, would be expected to exemplify the virtues of their parents, and in doing so, their memories would *long endure.* The intention of the commandment then is also a directive to parents to be deserving of honor.

The placement of this utterance after those glorifying God teaches that God's supremacy in no way diminishes reverence to parents. Josephus would later allow: "The Torah ranks the honoring of parents second only to that of God... It requires respect to be paid by the young to all their elders because God is the most ancient of all."[6] If children don't maintain their parents' legacies, who will? And in doing so, they set an example for their own children.

VI.   You shall not murder.

VII. You shall not commit adultery

VIII. You shall not steal.

IX.   You shall not bear false witness against your neighbor.

X.   You shall not covet your neighbor's house; you shall not covet your neighbor's wife, or his male or female slave, or his ox or his ass, or anything that is your neighbor's.

The final five are the "do not" utterances; the first four of these are straightforward and require no interpretation, but the last is less direct and requires explanation. It is unique in two important aspects.

The first is the repetition of the phrase, "You shall not covet," which may be rendered, "You shall not desire." The prior four are concise; this one repeats the leading phrase stressing its importance.

The repetition may be understood as taking a second look or a second desire. Recalling the incident of Joseph and Potiphar's wife, it would have been only human for Potiphar's wife to have noticed Joseph and considered him attractive. The problem was she looked again, desiring him more than once. That's what caused the problem.

It's human nature to desire things we don't have; the tenth utterance confronts the obsession to posses.

Its second key aspect is more subtle and existential, because it further highlights the need of emphasis in the repetition of the key word *covet*. The utterance is directed solely to the ethical behavior of the individual in a context so internalized as to be unenforceable as a law.

In speculating on its origin, it is reasonable to assume that Moses was disheartened by the envy and acquisitiveness in the royal court, in striking contrast to the impoverished Hebrew slaves who toiled endlessly and received no material reward for their efforts. Since he must have found it distressful to observe petty jealousies among the affluent who obsessed over possessions. Pharaoh's fixation on creating his own memorial in buildings and statuary would have been abhorrent to Moses.

It is also likely that he witnessed sibling rivalry among the daughters of Jethro. Perhaps, of more immediate concern, he observed greed and envy among those who had just been liberated, and Moses did his best to eliminate it.

Taken from, The Anchor Bible Dictionary, "I am the Lord your God, who brought you out of the land of Egypt..." reminds man that his outer liberty was given to him by God, and the tenth word, "You shall not covet" reminds him that he himself must achieve his inner liberty.[7]

Legal systems cannot succeed if they are only based on law enforcement. People must innately desire to act justly even where there is no law. What chaos we would have on our streets if drivers slowed down only when a cop was in sight. They must drive with caution mostly for their own protection and genuine concern for others. Consider how carefully drivers enter an intersection when a traffic light is not functioning and no officer is there to direct traffic.

Sir Fletcher Norton, an eighteenth century barrister, expressed it succinctly: "The greatness of a nation resides not in obedience to laws but in conventions that were not obligations."

The tenth utterance affirms that passion cannot be vanquished by decree. Hence, the corollary that no judicial system can be effective without individuals being existentially responsible for their own thoughts and actions. From the *Sayings of the Fathers*: "Who is strong? He who controls his desires."

> All the people witnessed the thunder and lightning, the blare of the horn and the mountain smoking; and when the people saw

it, they fell back and stood at a distance. "You speak to God," they said to Moses, "and we will obey; but let not God speak to us lest we die."

Exodus 20:15–17

The Hebrew phrase *aseret ha-devarim* (literally "the ten words") is taken from Exodus 34:28. The Utterances are even better known as the Ten Commandments. As much as I prefer "utterances" because the first of the ten in the Hebrew Bible is in the form of a statement, in deference to conformity from this time on they will be referred to as *commandments*.[8]

The Ten Commandments have been quoted precisely and completely from the JPS 1991 Torah Commentary (Exodus 20:1–14), with one modification derived from personal preference. In the second commandment, the Hebrew *chesed* is rendered "steadfast love" rather than "kindness." Many scholars contend the biblical denotation of *chesed* is to be taken as "constancy." In this particular context, the stronger rendering "steadfast love" is, I believe, more effective.[g]

There is some question as to who spoke each utterance. In the first and second, it is said that God spoke directly in the first person, and thereafter, he spoke through Moses. These uncertainties prompted Franz Rosenzweig to say that, "In the end, one who wishes to believe in the reality of the theophany, and yet wants to take account of all literary and historical

---

g   Buber/Rosenzweig German translation uses **true,** loyal, faithful.

difficulties, will have to conclude that all the people themselves experienced immediately, and not through mediation, was God's overwhelming presence... The words themselves came to them through Moses."[9]

They embody the concept expressed in the previous chapter of God giving the Israelites the choice to become *His treasured people* if only they would accept His commandments. The implication is the existential act of choosing what they as individual were to become.

BOOK OF THE COVENANT

As a body, the commandments are an introduction to the more specific laws that follow similar to the preamble that precedes the constitution of the United States. These laws known as the Book of the Covenant refer to worship, serfs, capital and non-capital offenses, property, and moral and religious duties. Only several of these laws will be presented to give the reader a flavor of their character, since these ordinances were contemporaneous with life in the ancient near-east.

Most of these laws bear a similarity to the laws of Hammurabi circa 1750 BCE, which Moses may have learned in his Egyptian school. However, the laws concerning strangers and slaves were unique to The Covenant.

> Therefore, you shall not make any gods of silver, nor shall you make for yourselves gods of gold. Make for me an altar of earth and sacrifice on it your burnt offerings… in every place where I cause My name to be mentioned I will come to you and bless you.
>
> Exodus 20:21

When you acquire a Hebrew slave he shall serve
six years; in the seventh year he shall go free.

Exodus 21:1

Slavery was the accepted norm in the ancient
Near East and was not forbidden for practical
reasons. However, now, in contrast to the experience
of the Israelites in Egypt, humane consideration was
mandated. This limited liability provision had the dual
effects of promulgating ethical behavior and revealing
God's compassion for all humankind.

The text continues to deplore Egyptian cruelty,
suggesting that a sensible judgment should not exceed
the value of a loss. We encounter the expression of "an
eye for an eye." According to rabbinic interpretation
this was to be taken as the monetary value of an eye
for the loss of an eye, but no more than an equivalent
value. Apparently, the Egyptians were often guilty of
cruel and unusual punishment exceeding the value of
the loss.

This concept was taken from Mesopotamian and
Hittite laws where monetary values were put on the
values of an eye, an ear, a tooth, an arm, and any other
number of body parts and injuries.

The problem is "an eye for an eye" is too often
taken literally, suggesting that if someone sustains an
injury inflicted by another, an identical injury in return
is appropriate compensation. Fortunately, this is no
longer common practice.

The Torah is even more judiciously generous: "When
a man strikes the eye of his slave, male or female, and

destroys it, he shall let him go free on account of his eye" (Exodus 21:26).

Rabbinic literature abounds with discussions of the legal intricacies, one of which is *the fine must be commensurate with the wealth of the offending party*.[1]

Concern for the stranger becomes more compelling each time it's repeated—actually, thirty-six times in the Torah—here, twice in different formats:

> You shall not wrong a stranger or oppress him, for you were strangers in the land of Egypt.
>
> Exodus 22:20

> You shall not oppress a stranger, for you know the feelings of the stranger, having yourselves been strangers in the land of Egypt.
>
> Exodus 23:9

It may have been that Moses had great empathy for strangers having been a stranger himself in the court of Pharaoh and the land of Midian. Concern for the stranger became the touchstone of biblical justice.

Cynthia Ozick makes an important reference to feelings for the stranger, expressed here and elsewhere in the Torah, in *Metaphor and Memory*: "Without the metaphor of memory and history, we cannot imagine the life of the other. We cannot imagine what it is to be someone else."[2] The corollary becomes the imperative: showing kindness to strangers implies we show no less than kindness to those we know.

From *The Torah, A Modern Commentary*: "To persons constantly aware of their relationship to God, Holiness is understood to be not only a moral outlook but a total life style."[3]

> Teach me Your way, O Lord;
> I will walk in your truth;

Psalm 86:11

> You shall be Holy people to Me.

Exodus 22:30

ALONE ATOP THE MOUNTAIN

The next morning an altar was set up at the foot of the mountain.

> Now the presence of the Lord appeared in the sight of the Israelites as a consuming fire on top of the mountain. Moses went inside the cloud and ascended the mountain; and Moses remained on the mountain forty days and forty nights.
>
> Exodus 24:17–18

Moses' brief round trips up and down Mount Sinai were now history. He was to begin a period of forty days in God's presence at the mountaintop committed to strategic planning. The people were to remain encamped at the base of Sinai, presumably awed by the consuming fire above as a reminder of YHVH's presence.

But they were not to remain there indefinitely. It was intended they would soon begin the arduous journey to the Promised Land. Moses was concerned that once they were separated from the mountain, they would feel detached from God's presence.[1] Further, he questioned how long they would remain faithful to their commitment that "all that the Lord has spoken we will do!" (Exodus 19:8).

God, who had provided the commandments and laws, had not been a complete abstraction. Although unseen, His presence was spectacularly evident in moments of dark clouds, thunder, and lightning. However, it was anticipated the harmony of those moments would turn to dissonance without the positive reinforcement of things the people could see, touch, and feel.

> The Lord spoke to Moses, saying: "Tell the Israelite people to bring me gifts; you shall accept gifts for me from every person whose heart so moves him… And let them make me a sanctuary that I may dwell among them.
>
> Exodus 25:1–8

The idea of each person making gifts to God for the creation of a sanctuary and paying a modest, uniform tax for its maintenance was a stroke of genius. Equal commitment would enforce the idea that each person is unique and equal in the sight of God.

From *The Torah, A Modern Commentary*: "In Egyptian slavery, Israel made buildings for the pharaohs, now they would be privileged to expend their labor for God's sake."[2] Collectively, gifts, taxes, and physical efforts would serve to enhance the feeling of the Lord's presence.

This chapter's title is meant to emphasize there was no one else present; Moses was alone in the presence of the Invisible. God spoke, and Moses listened.

In summary, God gave detailed instructions to Moses for the building of a portable sanctuary, a tent of meeting, also referred to as the tabernacle, *Mishkan*. Holiness was the touchstone of the tabernacle, which was to be a tangible representation of God's invisible presence abiding among the people wherever they might travel. It was a concept, novel in the ancient Middle East, in which deities took permanent residence on mountain tops.

The ark to contain the tables of the law was to be the most important furnishing of the tabernacle. The materials of construction were specified as acacia wood overlaid with pure gold inside and out. Poles of gold-covered acacia wood would be attached on each side for ease of mobility. When positioned in the tabernacle, the ark would be in the most elaborately decorated section, appropriately designated the Holy of holies.

Other artifacts were specified to adorn the tabernacle, most notably a gold lamp stand of six branches, two altars, one for incense and one for burnt offerings, cherubim[h] and curtains. The instructions described in detail how they were to be made and the materials of construction, but gave no inkling of what they should look like. The design was delegated to the craftsmen and women.

Moses knew that the men were not all brick-makers, indeed, some were skilled artisans. There were women who could sew and weave to create decorative fabrics

---

[h]   A vague term referring to fanciful composite winged beings. (Anchor Bible Dictionary, page 899).

and garments. Several had talents that had caught the attention of Egyptian royalty who used them to design artifacts for the palaces and sacred places.

From living in Egypt, Moses knew that a sanctuary required functionaries trained to perform sacraments, sacrifices, and other sacral duties. For this God chose Aaron and his sons to be ordained as priests. The designs of their garments were not specified, only the materials of their fabrication. They were to be highly ornamented, and, lacking specifics, the designers were likely to draw on past experience to create vestments familiar to the Israelites.

God further instructed Moses to take a census and assess the people equitably to reaffirm the importance of equality:

> When you take a census of the Israelite people… each shall pay the Lord a ransom for himself on being enrolled… every one shall pay a half-shekel… as an offering to the Lord… The rich shall not pay more and the poor shall not pay less… to the service of the Tent of Meeting; it shall serve the Israelites as a reminder before the Lord.
>
> Exodus 30:11–16

This passage concludes with a powerful reaffirmation of the importance of the Sabbath. Even though the tasks of building the tabernacle and its appurtenances are divine commands, the Sabbath was to take unconditional precedence. God concludes with these words for Moses to retell to the Israelites:

Just as I have commanded you, they shall do…
Nevertheless, you must keep My Sabbaths, for
this is a sign between Me and you throughout
the ages, that you may know that I, the Lord,
have consecrated you. You shall keep the
Sabbath, for it is Holy to you. He who profanes
it shall be put to death; whoever does work
on it, that person shall be cut off from among
his kin… The Israelite people shall keep the
Sabbath throughout the ages as a covenant for
all time.

Exodus 31:13–16

When He finished speaking with him on
Mount Sinai, He gave Moses the two tablets of
the Pact, stone tablets inscribed with the finger
of God.

Exodus 31:18

During forty days on the mountain, only what God
said is recorded in the Torah. There was no interchange
of expression, only God spoke and Moses took notes.
But with no witnesses, we have only Moses' version
of what transpired, or perhaps, what he wanted the
Israelites to hear.

If we read the full text, we find many disquieting
ideas, especially matters pertaining to sacrifices, the
severe punishment of death for profaning the Sabbath,
and the tablets inscribed with the finger of God.
The modern reader may be disturbed by the literal
implication that these words were spoken by God
to Moses.

For a different perspective, we need to consider the thinking of Rabbi Samuel Sandmel, professor of Bible and Hellenistic literature at the Hebrew Union College for years. Rabbi Sandmel couched his ideas in a novel, *Alone Atop the Mountain*.[3] Religious and philosophic thinkers, as with Sartre, often presented new ideas in fictional form to make them more accessible.

His biblical fiction presents Moses as the storyteller relating the Grand Narrative from his point of view. Rabbi Daniel Syme once told me Rabbi Sandmel shocked many of his students when he put words, such as the following, into the mouth of Moses:

> Alone atop the mountain, above the clouds, I experienced cold and hunger and loneliness, and anxiety about my purpose. I prayed to Him from time to time, and He answered my prayers... I found a huge flat rock, and on it I chiseled the Ten Words He had spoken.
>
> I was determined that I should not be thought of as ruler, or king, that I wanted there to be an office which I would never hold. My laws must never be mine, must never come from the imposition of a tyrant of his will on a cowed and subdued people... In the interest of my role as the framer of their laws, I felt the need for a high priest, while I could always remain Moses without a title.
>
> I was proud of the clarity of the laws. I was proud of the regulations for worship... How wondrously I had labored, how wondrously I had achieved! When ideas eluded me, I prayed to Him, and in His own way He answered,

and I knew from His answering that He too approved what I had done. Now it was time to return.

I present Sandmel's views as an alternative to the traditional acceptance of the biblical words "and the Lord spoke to Moses." They suggest a new slant on the Grand Narrative. On the other hand, they may strengthen more conventional ideas—ideas delicately etched in the mind's eye by a loving parent, teacher, or grandparent. An optical prism reveals the colors of the rainbow—an existential prism reveals a rainbow of memories.

Harold Bloom, who calls himself a cultural Jew, finds memories inescapable: "My orthodox Judaic childhood lingers in me as an awe of YHVH." David, my bar mitzvah student, will always remember his religious school teacher who proffered the simile of God's resembling the wind and the memory of his bar mitzvah as well, just as I will always remember David.

Consider an example of memory in another context. It makes no difference, which of several scholarly hints, one accepts as to the magnitude of the Exodus—two million, ten thousand, or small groups leaving Egypt over an extended period of time.[4] The context of memory often serves to select one choice of the three, satisfying a comfort factor that cannot be dismissed.

In briefly reviewing Genesis, we saw that a major theme woven throughout the book is the disappearance of God. Recalling my theatrical metaphor, in the end, God sat in a box seat from which point His imminence could be only felt by those on the stage. He could neither be seen nor heard.

Richard Eliot Friedman extensively developed this theme in his book *The Hidden Face of God*: "The deity disappears in the course of the narrative. The Hebrew Bible uses a more metaphorical phrase, *God hides His face*." Bloom takes a more extreme position, jokingly asserting that God should be "convicted for desertion."[5]

Through the eyes of Sandmel, Friedman, and Bloom, we may now see the biblical expression "stone tablets inscribed with the finger of God" to be an elegant metaphor.

The strategic plan for the construction of the sanctuary and the ark, the making of the sacral vessels, and the advancement of Aaron and his sons to the priesthood was prepared for implementation. The commandments were put in writing. Moses was ready to go down and rejoin the people.

> And let them make Me a sanctuary That I may dwell among them.
>
> Exodus 25:8

BETRAYAL

When Rabbi Lieberman spoke of God as the most tragic character in the Bible, he had in mind more than the disappointments He suffered from setbacks in Genesis. At the time when God and Moses were putting the final touches on their strategic plan, the people below were experiencing a collective anxiety attack. The fracas at the base of the mountain was another monumental tragedy.

When they saw that "Moses was so long in coming down from the mountain, the people gathered against Aaron" and insisted he make them a god who could go before them. Aaron took their gold jewelry and other artifacts and made them into a calf before which they offered sacrifices, drank, danced, and declared: "This is your god, O Israel, who brought you out of the land of Egypt!" (Exodus 32:4).

Their infidelity made God angry. Before Moses departed from the mountain God threatened to destroy the people. Moses, in an eloquent forensic style that would impress a modern-day jury, persuaded God to relent. Moses understood, as my friend Rabbi Dannel Schwartz once opined, "It was easier to take the people out of Egypt, than to take Egypt out of the people."

The argument between God and Moses raises more interesting questions. Was God's anger consistent with his redeeming the people from Pharaoh's yoke and choosing them to be His "treasured possession among all the peoples"? Was it not likely Moses exaggerated the argument to report to the people that he had interceded with God on their behalf?

Moses then went down the mountain bearing the stone tablets inscribed with the law to see what was going on. The first individual he met when he arrived near the scene was Joshua who said, "There is a cry of war in the camp." To which Moses replied, "It is the sound of song that I hear" (Exodus 32:18).

When he saw the calf and the dancing, he appeared to be enraged and hurled the tablets to the ground, shattering them. He *burned* the calf to powder, strewed it on the water, and made them drink it. The Psalmist said in vivid perspective: "They have exchanged their glory for the image of a bull that feeds on grass" (Psalm 106:20).

Was Moses acting in a fit of anger a façade? I think he had already anticipated such a problem when God proposed erecting a tabernacle. But perhaps not quite so soon.

He understood and was prepared to deal with the people's proclivity to revert to their previous religious experiences. He was also aware that his extended absence might have been traumatic. Avivah Zornberg equates it to the emotion an infant experiences when separated from its mother.[1]

When he saw the people dancing and singing before the calf, he surmised that Aaron had executed a clever ploy. He knew Aaron was aware that the Egyptians did not worship animals. In the iconography of the ancient Middle East, animal objects were used as footstools upon which gods sat, not as objects of worship.[2]

It follows that Aaron contrived to appease the people's thirst for a tangible object of worship by fashioning a footstool without an occupant. The calf, instead of symbolizing a deity, represented a place where the Invisible might be present. And who were they to identify as the occupant of that animal footstool: Moses.

For another interesting hypothesis, consider the following midrash:

> Moses broke the tablets out of his love for Israel, for as long as they did not know the Torah they would be judged less harshly. God consoled him saying, "The second tablets will contain much more material, laws, midrash, and legends."[3]

Moses' dramatic destruction of the tablets was, most likely, a contrived exhibition of anger, not a genuine emotional outburst. Thus forcing the people to drink the dust of the calf was intended as a punishment to reassure loyalty to him, their earthbound leader.

His display of anger, demonstrated by destroying the tablets, was a crowd pleaser. We've all seen the apparently irate football coach rip the headphones from his head and smash them to the turf to display his displeasure to the fans, the players, and the officials.

In an apparent state of rage, Moses rebuked Aaron for his complicity in the sin that had been committed, and he commissioned the Levites, quoting God's authority, to put to death those who had sinned. "Some three thousand of the people died that day" (Exodus 32:28).

Interestingly, Aaron was not put to death and was also not deprived of his impending appointment by God to become the high priest—sure signs of Moses' understanding that Aaron was caught in a trap from which he did his best to extricate himself.

I have trouble accepting the killing of the people because they violated two of the commandments, the prohibition against worshipping any deity but YHVH and the prohibition against worshiping graven images. It seems unlikely that Moses, who had anticipated how difficult it would be to take Egypt out of the people, would have inflicted the ultimate punishment. As a practical matter, he expected further encounters with the Amalekites and would need every able bodied man.

My existential prerogative rejects as reality the inhumanity of such senseless killing by Moses, even worse as the alleged will of God. God would have been violating his own law that the punishment should not exceed the magnitude of the crime—"an eye for an eye."

With no coaching from the Lord, Moses went down and, in his own way, confronted the crime of idolatry. The essential focus is on Moses' emerging independence as a leader in the real world of human frailty. He sought to preserve the Lord's gift of freedom of choice; to stand in awe of him, but to refuse to comply. This is only the beginning. As we proceed we'll continue to see more moments of non-compliance on the part of Moses.

> The next day Moses said to the people, "You have been guilty of a great sin. Yet I will now go up to the Lord; perhaps I may win forgiveness for your sin."
>
> Exodus 32:30

Upon his return up the mountain, Moses' first words to God were a plea to forgive the people; and if God were to choose otherwise, he, Moses, would rather die. God proffered a compromise. Because of their collective infidelity, he refused to join in the midst of *the stiff necked people*, but, instead, would delegate an angel to lead them. In retaliation, God sent a plague upon the people for what they did.

The episode of the golden calf was so physically violent and emotionally wrenching that it has gotten unwarranted attention in movies, religious schools, and interpretive ink. I can think of no better example than my own stream of consciousness reaction, mentioned earlier, upon first seeing a mountain alleged to be Sinai. You may recall how I envisioned multitudes riotously celebrating at its base.

At that moment, I was thinking of it as a monumental heresy. Later, I saw through the eyes of Hamlet how evasive memory can be after as brief a span as forty days. Shakespeare's prince bemoaned the marriage of his mother to his uncle, the king, after a like time span: "A little month, or ere those shoes were old with which she followed my poor father's body, like Niobe, all tears."[4]

As seen through my prism, with Hamlet's prompting, I have taken an oblique view of Moses' reaction to the infidelity. Most people side with God. You will find an interesting discussion of that point of view by reading Avivah Zornberg's chapter, "The Golden Calf: Fire in the Bones" in her reflections on *Exodus: The Particles of Rapture.*

> He would have destroyed them Had not Moses
> His chosen one Confronted Him in the breech
> To avert His destructive wrath.
>
> Psalm 106:23

AWE AND TRANSITION

The Grand Narrative relates the journey of the Israelites from bondage in Egypt to a life of freedom, a spiritual journey from darkness into light. The meaning is enriched by the development of the participants on the biblical stage, particularly Moses whose maturation is a major subtheme of the Grand Narrative. Only God epitomizes constancy, appearing to change only in the perceptions of those who experience Him.

Moses exemplified Sartre's first principle of existentialism: "Man is nothing else but what he makes of himself... he is conscious of imagining himself as being in the future."[1]

Sartre had a more elegant phrase for this point: "to realize one's authentic self." The process is the nucleus of the passages we are about to discuss beginning with Exodus 33. This brief segment centers on a tipping point in Moses' life; his relation to God.

We pick up the narrative as Moses pitched a tent outside the camp, which became known as the Tent of Meeting, so called because it was there he would meet with the Lord. It was a temporary substitute for the tabernacle as described previously. "The Lord would speak to Moses face to face, as a man speaks to his neighbor" (Exodus 33:11).

Since Moses thought like an existentialist, we must pause to look at the existential nature of the Hebrew *panim al panim*, freely translated here, "face to face"— literally translated, "faces on faces"—not quite the same implication. In English parlance, we employ such idioms as meeting someone face-to-face or discussing a matter face-to-face, both singular.

But in Hebrew, the language of the Bible, there is no singular for *panim*, no noun for only one face. The Hebrew language recognizes the reality that everyone has a multiplicity of faces. Even within the family, a mother is seen differently by each sibling, her husband, and, indeed, her own mother.

In Buber's view: "Whenever two people interact, each has four different faces: the image of oneself as one wishes to appear to the other; the way in which one actually appears to the other; the image each has of himself or herself; and the bodily self."[2]

Often, we try to present our genuine selves only to have such images modified by the existential prisms of others. Such alterations reflect the other's partial image of someone else, a personal contact of similar appearance or personality.

A great gift of the Hebrew language is that it's seasoned with existential flavoring. *Panim* is not unique in this respect. The noun *chayim*, translated "life," also has no singular, connoting—just as our faces appear in various contexts—our lives are perceived differently by all those who know us.

Unlike faces that have a degree of malleability, they can be varied to adapt to situations, existentially our lives are in part what we are able to make them. Buber held a dynamic concept of person. Rather than being made up of fixed qualities that define his or her character, a person is in a continual state of becoming.[3]

A similar case can be made for the Hebrew word for *heaven, shamayim* (literally, heavens). Surely, there is no singular idea of heaven.

This circuitous linguistic trip was necessary before returning to the idiom *face to face* or, if one prefers, *panim al panim.* In the Bible *faces* is frequently used as an idiom for God's presence, which makes the sense of the plural even more worthy of attention.

In a commentary, Cassuto argues, "Moses was not like one who sees visions, or falls into a trance; he was in possession of his senses and heard the sound of words."[4] *Seeing* in the sense of listening to, feeling the presence of.

This insight again brings to mind the encounter at the burning bush in which God was unique in terms of his constancy. "I will be that which I will be," reliable and steadfast. All humankind from limited viewpoints would experience a continuous progression to "see" more and more of his constant presence. And so it was with Moses. During the intervening several months, Moses had lived intimately in the presence of YHVH, aware of his own changing awareness of the Invisible.

During that same period, God had witnessed Moses' development as a person, a leader and God's emissary. His crowning achievement was his loyalty to the people despite their heresy and God's antipathy. Zornberg called it "the fire in his bones." The evolution of Moses is revealed in the following dialogue:

> Moses said to the Lord, "… You have said, 'I have singled you out by name, and you have, indeed, gained my favor.' Now if I have truly gained Your favor, pray let me know Your ways, that I may know You and continue in Your favor."
>
> Exodus 33:12–13

The words of God to Moses, "I have singled you out by name," are applied to no one else in the Bible. The expression connotes the emergence of a close, exclusive, and unique association.

Moses, once again, appealed to God to lead the people; and this was God's response:

> And the Lord said to Moses, "I will do this thing that you have asked, for you have truly gained My favor and I have singled you out by name." [Moses] said, "Oh, let me behold Your presence!" And [God] answered, "I will make all My goodness pass before you, and I will proclaim before you the name YHVH, that I show favor to whom I show favor, that I show mercy to whom I show mercy. But, you cannot see My face, for man may not see Me and live."
>
> Exodus 33:17–20

The similarity of this dialogue to the dialogue at the bush is no accident. Buber discussed the symmetry from several perspectives: substance, meter, and style. If repetition of key words was a stylistic means of stressing importance, it follows that the repetition of a fundamental idea would make the idea expressly germane.

To add further emphasis, both passages are acknowledged as from the same writer—the first of the four writers.[i] Today, we might say they flowed from the same pen. Having come from the same source further enhances their noteworthiness compared to repetitious biblical texts that flowed from different pens to convey individual biases, but were not necessarily intended for emphasis. In substance, the symmetry of all these factors gives rise to the implication that the passages were to be interpreted together.

Moses showed humility by not asking God his name, as he did at the bush. This time, he sought to discover God's essence through an exclusively individual experience. God's response was less elliptical than the former "I will be what I will be," which, in Buber's commentary, can only be understood as an avoidance of the question—an explanation, not a name.[5]

God offered the assurance "I will make all My goodness pass before you." With an understanding of

---

[i]   To avoid confusion I have, until now, avoided reference to the generally accepted conclusion of scholars, known as the Higher Criticism, that the Torah is a composite of several sources. The subject is lucidly presented in two books by Richard Elliott Friedman: *Who Wrote The Bible* and *The Hidden Book of the Bible*.

existentialism, it becomes apparent that the meaning of this beautifully crafted phrase was that God's abundance of goodness would always be present, but that within the finite limits of experience only a passing glimpse would be apparent.

Ever mindful of God's constancy, Buber observed, "It is not God who changes, only the theophany—the manifestation of the Divine in man's symbol-creating mind—until no symbol is adequate any longer, and none is needed."[6]

As if in answer to Moses' previous question, God revealed, "I will proclaim before you the name YHVH [Lord]." The Lord made a similar declaration many years later to the prophet Isaiah, "I am YHVH, that is My name" (Isaiah 42:8).

The question arises, why now and not at the bush? In the ancient Near East, a name was meant to be a designation for the essence of the being. In Exodus 3, Moses was not ready to grasp the essence of God; now, he was.

Further, without a name, a person is unapproachable. Since God and Moses now speak

Face-to-face, God has appropriately disclosed his name.

> That I show favor to whom I show favor, That
> I show mercy to whom I show mercy.
>
> (Exodus 33:19, from Everett Fox translation)

These words recall the earlier answer to Moses in Exodus 4:13. God's meaning here is that "I choose to whom I will reveal myself." Anticipating repetition, it was in this context a message to the people that Moses' responsibility was that of an emissary of the Lord— through Moses, their reconciliation with God had been accomplished.

"You cannot see My face, for man cannot see Me and live." This phrase is interesting because Moses did not make such a request. It was probably intended to reinforce the infidelity of the calf, strengthening the idea that the Invisible could reveal only his presence. Zornberg tells us "that to encounter God's face is possible only within language."[7]

The language may seem strange to us today, but it would have been familiar to the emigrants from Egypt. They would have been familiar with a notion of the ancient Near East not to stare at gods for fear of death, reinforced by Pharaoh Ikhnaton's religion based exclusively on one god, that of the sun, Aton-Ra.[8] Staring at the sun at any time is, of course, certainly never a good idea. Even in Greek myth, Semele was reduced to ashes when she saw Zeus in full splendor.

Cassuto gives a more traditional explanation: "To perceive the face of My glory is beyond the power of man's comprehension throughout the days of his life upon earth. You will be able to perceive only My works and to discern from them some of My attributes, but you will be unable to comprehend my essential nature."[9]

> And the Lord said, "See there is a place near Me. Station yourself on the rock and as My presence passes by, I will put you in a cleft of the rock and shield you with My hand until I

have passed by. Then I will take my hand away
and you will see my back; but My face must not
be seen."

Exodus 33:21–23

The metaphor of being placed in *a cleft of the rock*
is similar to Plato's allegory of the cave. We visited
the latter during our field trip of ideas giving rise to
existentialism. I am not suggesting Plato caught the
idea from Moses. Although not impossible, Plato made
no reference to deities; it is more likely that their great
minds thought alike.

From within the recesses of a cave, one has only
a fleeting peek at what passes by the opening to the
outside. In the present metaphor, it was God's back; but
in Plato's, it was shadows on the wall.

A brief look may be all one has to form a perception.
The text prompted Sarna's comment, "No human
being can ever penetrate the ultimate mystery of God's
Being. Only a glimpse of the divine reality is possible,
even for Moses."[10]

God then asked Moses to carve two tablets, like the
ones he shattered, upon which he would inscribe the
words. The next morning, carrying the blank stones,
Moses went up Mount Sinai to meet the Lord who
came down in a cloud and proclaimed:

> YHVH! YHVH! A God showing mercy and
> favor, slow to anger, abundant in steadfast love
> and faithfulness, extending steadfast love to
> the thousandth generation, forgiving iniquity,
> transgression and sin; yet He does not remit all

punishment, but visits the iniquity of parents upon children and children's children, upon the third and fourth generation.

Exodus 34:6–7

These words were God's response to Moses' plea to "know your ways" and "behold your *imageless* Presence." Chanted in Hebrew by the cantor before the open arc and repeated in translation by the rabbi, they play a prominent role in the Reform Synagogue High Holy Day and Festival services. Sarna explains, "These words, encompassing the Thirteen Attributes of God, are the essence of God's character and to know them is to achieve a higher conception of the deity."[11]

Our attention is immediately drawn to the repetition of God's name, *YHVH! YHVH!* Our sages tell us there is no needless repetition in the Torah. For an existential understanding, we turn to Buber.

Although answers are not always readily apparent in Buber's writings, he was explicit in his seminal treatise, "I and Thou," stating, "Of course God is the wholly Other; but He is also the wholly Present."[12] Relating Buber's words to the present text, I would take them to mean that the first YHVH represents the God that one does not know, has not yet experienced; the second YHVH, the God one has already come to know.

Buber was only one of the many thousands of scholars and rabbis who have attempted to pierce the mystery of the repetition of the name. Thinking existentially would lead us to believe that the mystery is the message.

Another option is to investigate the name by using a lens, instead of a prism, to look at the letters and the interstices between them. The configuration of Hebrew letters forming God's name are unutterable; they are not intended to be pronounced.

Rabbi Lawrence Kushner, who is committed to the interpretation of Hebrew words, explains the letters YHVH in this way: "Not because of the Holiness they evoke, but because they are all vowels, and you cannot pronounce all vowels at once without risking respiratory injury. They are frequently pronounced 'Yahveh,' but in truth they are unutterable… They are also the root letters of the word 'to be.'"[j]

We have come full circle back to the enigma at the bush. However, in the present sense the name, reiterated, precedes the remaining attributes. It apparently is intended to be conjoined with what follows in the sense of "I will be merciful, I will show favor."

> He made known His ways to Moses, His deeds
> to the children of Israel.
> The Lord is compassionate and gracious,
> Slow to anger, abounding in steadfast love.
>
> Psalm 103:7-8

> Moses hastened to bow low to the ground in
> homage, and said, "If I have gained Your favor,
> O Lord, pray, let the Lord go in our midst, even

---

[j]   The first use of the term "Ten Commandments" in the Torah.

though this is a stiff-necked people. Pardon our iniquity and our sin, and take us for Your own!"

Exodus 34:8–9

God then committed to a new covenant and to work wonders for the people. He set forth a concise body of laws, for the most part specific to the ensuing journey and other laws eschewing idolatry.

And he was there with the Lord forty days and forty nights; he ate no bread and drank no water; and he wrote down on the tablets the terms of the covenant, the Ten Commandments.[13]

And as Moses came down from the mountain bearing the two tablets of the Pact, Moses was not aware that the skin of his face was radiant, since he had spoken with Him. Aaron and all the Israelites saw that the skin of Moses' face was radiant; and they shrank from coming near him.

Exodus 34:27–31

"The skin of his face was radiant." We must perish the thought that the change in Moses' face was sunburn acquired during his tenure on the mountain. The expression "was radiant" is the English rendition of the Hebrew *keren*, literally "rays of light."

Sarna speaks of it as "a reflection of the divine radiance." It is more understandable as a metaphor for a mystical experience. Does it conflict with the quotation from Cassuto who contended Moses "does not see visions or fall into trances"?

The probable answer is found in a study by neurologist Andrew Newberg, MD, and his associates on brain science and the biology of belief. Their brain studies document the activity of the brain when God is experienced: "Mysticism is the name of that organic process which involves the perfect consummation of the love of God: the achievement here and now of the immortal heritage of man. It is the art of establishing his own conscious relation with the Absolute... An uplifting sense of genuine spiritual union with something larger than the self."[14]

It is not something remote from human experience. They suggest, "Humans are natural mystics blessed with an inborn genius for effortless self-transcendence. If you have ever lost yourself in a beautiful piece of music or felt swept away by a rousing patriotic speech, you have tasted the essence of mystical union."[15] Buber called these experiences "thought moments"; Virginia Woolf spoke of them as "moments of being."

One may wonder if this has anything to do with existentialism. The authors resolve any ambiguity. "All perceptions exist in the mind. The earth beneath your feet, the chair you're sitting in, the book you hold in your hand may all seem unquestionably real, but they are known to you only as secondhand neurological perceptions, as blips and flashes racing along the neural pathways inside your skull....

"Neurologically, the mind has the power to grant meaning and substance to its own perceptions, thoughts and beliefs, and to regard them as meaningful."[16]

The subject of mystical experience is so germane to the thesis of our discussion that several personal anecdotes will, I hope, reinforce the study. Mystical unions become existential experiences when they become part of us, when they are characterized by their enduring nature, their persistent recurrence, or when they turn into elements of our being.

❑ In an effort to answer Sartre's question "Where is Beethoven's Seventh Symphony today?" discussed earlier, I found the subtle E minor theme of the slow movement resonating in my mind long after I finished writing about it. I know I shall never forget the mesmerizing effect of the repetitious rhythm of the second movement awash in the color of orchestral harmonies, leaving no doubt as to where Beethoven's seventh is today.

❑ A friend, who had obviously spent hours on the psychoanalytic couch once asked me, "What is the first thought that comes to mind when you think of your mother?" Without a moment's hesitation, I recalled a particular occasion telling my mother I loved her. The recollection came to me as a total surprise. I don't think I had ever given much thought to the conversation. I must have been six or seven and seated in the front seat of the car beside her. Unprompted by the conversation, I gave vent to my feelings. Triggered by my friend's question, the memory emerged from hiding to reside in my consciousness, I think, forever.

❏ I met Arlene at dinner on her first day at the University of Michigan in Ann Arbor. She had a twinkle in her eye, an infectious laugh, a warm smile, and I could sense the warmth of her inner beauty. I was sufficiently mature to identify it as an instant infatuation, but I felt that, even if we never met again, I would in no way ever be the same. To never meet again was out of the question; I knew where she lived and I had her phone number. The instant infatuation was rewarded by a loving, enduring relationship—we were married two years later.

Newberg would describe Moses' and my experiences as observable neurological activity. A brain scan would reveal them as a hot spot on "the orientation association area of the brain."

The question remains, why was this particular sojourn of Moses on the mountain different from the others? Prior to the calf incident, everything was working for him—the liberation was a huge success, and the people had committed to the covenant. Now, despite his tacit acceptance of what took place with the calf, he was disheartened and unsure.

Rabbi Sandmel showed uncanny insight getting into Moses' head without a brain scan: "I found myself believing that they had sinned against me. I told myself that this was wrong, that this was the way of a Pharaoh who believed that in some way he was a god, and that

I must not think thoughts such as those; yet from time to time I thought them."[17]

Before the calf, Moses enjoyed collaboration with God; after the calf, he needed the reassurance of God's enduring presence.

Moses was like children who feel free and independent of their parents as long as things are going well. However, if they encounter adversity, sickness, a bad day in school, a discouraging social contact—traumas of discontinuity—there follow tipping points back to dependence and need for parental support. In Moses' words:

> You have said, "I have singled you out by name, and you have, indeed, gained My favor." Now if I have truly gained Your favor, pray let me know Your ways, that I may know You and continue in Your favor.
>
> Exodus 33:12–13

MAKING THE INVISIBLE VISIBLE

> Afterwards all the Israelites came near, and he
> instructed them concerning all that the Lord
> had imparted to him on Mount Sinai.
>
> Exodus 34:32

Did you ever wonder why, after his second forty-day sojourn on the mountain, Moses received a warm welcome upon his return? The answer is found by reading between the lines.

The preparation was significant. Before returning to the mountain, he prepared two blank stone tablets on which God would dictate his words for Moses to carve in stone. Before going up, he made clear how long he would be with God. Those who knew numbers could count the days. Aware of their short memories, Moses undoubtedly had a few words to say about the calf.

The experience of the calf validated the need to make the Invisible visible without violating the commandments.

> I will make all My goodness pass before you, and
> I will proclaim before you the name YHVH, that

I show favor to whom I show favor, that I show mercy to whom I show mercy. But, you cannot see My face, for no man can see Me and live.

Exodus 33:19–20

It seems like the thought of making the Invisible visible would be fraught with danger, because it might be taken literally. Moses was actually thinking in terms of seeing God with the inner eye. He strove to make this nuance crystal clear to the people.

Most likely, Moses was inspired by a plan of Pharaoh Ikhnaton who conceived of worshipping an invisible deity. Ikhnaton had in mind the rays of the sun, which become visible only when their light is either refracted or reflected, otherwise it is what scientists call white light—the apparent absence of colors.

And let them make Me a sanctuary that I may dwell among them.

Exodus 25:8

The idea of the tabernacle (*Mishkan*, in Hebrew) was to create a structure in which the Presence of YHVH could be experienced. The physical eye could see God's objective goodness in the ark, the tablets and other appurtenances of the tabernacle; the inner eye would then sense his subjective presence.

And they shall know that I, the Lord, am their God, who brought them out of the land of Egypt that I might dwell among them.

Exodus 29:46

Before Moses descended the mountain, God once again reminded him to instruct the people to keep the Sabbath. He did as he had been told when he gathered the Israelites together, but with one significant modification:

> These are the things that the Lord has commanded you to do: On six days work may be done, but on the seventh day you shall have a Sabbath of complete rest, Holy to the Lord; whoever does any work on it shall be put to death. You shall kindle no fire throughout your settlements on the Sabbath day.
>
> Exodus 35:1–3

Moses' caution to the people implied that sanctification of the Sabbath was to take priority over God's command to build the tabernacle. Moses feared that their enthusiasm for the task at hand might lead to a desecration of the Sabbath. He was advancing the idea that the Sabbath was more than a respite from work but a day of spiritual enhancement—in Ibn Ezra's words, "an island of Holiness in a turbulent sea of worldliness."[1]

But why the specific reference to not kindling fire? Was not the kindling of fire an obvious form of work? Since these particular words were not previously attributed to God, they must have come from Moses' remarkable understanding of human nature and deserve special consideration.

Moses might have intended what Zornberg called the "fire in the bones." In this case, the burning anxiety of creativity. The mental effort of focusing on creative ideas would have been an invasion of the "island of Holiness."

Moses continued with what the Lord had commanded:

> Take from among you gifts to the Lord; everyone whose *heart so moves him* shall bring them—gifts for the Lord: gold, silver and copper; blue, purple, and crimson yarns... [The list of materials goes on] And let all among you who are skilled come and make all that the Lord has commanded: the tabernacle, its tent and covering... the ark and its poles... the lampstand, the sacral vestments...
>
> So the whole community of the Israelites left Moses' presence. And everyone who excelled in ability and every one whose spirit moved him came, bringing offerings for the work of the Tent of Meeting... Men and women, all whose hearts moved them, all who would make an elevation offering of gold to the Lord came bringing brooches, earrings, rings and pendants—gold objects of all kinds.
>
> Exodus 35:10–22

Germane to the existential message is that the people were to give as their spirits and hearts moved them. Later, the Bible appropriately called them *freewill offerings*. There ensued an avalanche of gifts, *morning after morning*, expressing enthusiastic support for building the tabernacle until there was a superabundance. This gives credence to the violation of the Sabbath by kindling an actual or figurative fire.

One may wonder where all the finery came from. I failed to mention that before their escape the people had borrowed from their Egyptian neighbors objects of silver, gold, and clothing.

It is generally accepted that the tabernacle showed that God had forgiven Israel for the sin of the golden calf and that their unconstrained freewill offerings of gifts were in expiation for that sin.

On the other hand, is it not likely the idea of a tabernacle and its appurtenances were what the people were looking for when they made the calf? Bulls of stone or bronze were not objects of worship per se but bases on which idols were placed. Typically, in the ancient Near East, deities were enthroned in houses of their own with appropriate symbols and aromas to enhance the feeling of their presence. The people needed these familiar and tangible manifestations of a deity.

During the planning stage (Exodus 31:1–12), God allegedly told Moses about Bezalel[k] who was "endowed with a divine spirit of skill, ability and knowledge in every kind of craft" and similarly his assistant Oholiab (31:3). Now Moses told the people how God had *singled them out* to be in charge of the construction and to allocate the work effort of others with skills and abilities. It may be that Moses was avoiding responsibility in the event the appointments were not acceptable.

It is said that people came forward—those whose only work had been making bricks in Egypt—who felt they had a flair for more diverse tasks. It would

---

[k]   The meaning of the name Bezalel is "shadow of God."

have been the responsibility of Bezalel and Oholiab to instruct, nurture, and direct their efforts.

Much has been written about the artistic genius and creativity of Bezalel—the master craftsman among the riff-raff—whom God endowed with prodigious talent. A segment from one *midrash* has unique relevance:

> It is written, "Behold, I [God] have created the smith that blows the fire of coals...." When people began to praise him and everybody was saying that Bezalel had constructed the *Mishkan* [tabernacle] through his knowledge and understanding, the Holy One, blessed be He, said, "It was I who created and taught him. Behold, I have created the smith."[2]

It's not presumptive to believe that the reference to Bezalel as a smith was to be taken figuratively rather than metalurgically. It is acknowledged that his talent exceeded that of hammering red hot, malleable metal. The implication is that of the fire in his bones.

The Torah describes how the more skilled workers made the tabernacle. They made cloths of goat's hair to cover the tent, planks of acacia wood overlaid with gold for the walls and floor, cloths "of fine twisted linen... into which they worked a design of cherubim."

The primary object to be put in the tabernacle was the ark of the covenant to be placed in the center of the area designated the Holy of holies. It was crafted by Bezalel's own hands from acacia wood. It measured 45 x 27 x 27 inches and was overlaid with gold inside and out. He made poles of gold-covered acacia wood, which were inserted into gold rings on the sides for carrying the ark. The cover was of paramount importance. It was made of pure gold with hammered cherubim at each end. Their wings were spread out above to appear to shield the cover.

The references to cherubim in the tabernacle were important; they occur over ninety times in the Hebrew Bible and twice here. Described in various ways, they were all winged beings as depicted in ancient Near East art. Cherubim were said to constitute a resting place, or throne, for God's invisible presence.[3]

The text describes the other furnishings Bezalel designed and made: the lampstand [*menorah*] of pure gold consisting of a central shaft with three branches on each side, the incense altar of acacia wood overlaid with pure gold, the anointing oil, and the blended, aromatic incense.

When the work was completed, the people brought all the component parts, the appurtenances, and the vestal robes to Moses who blessed them for having done the Lord's work. On the first day of the second year, Moses supervised the erection of the tabernacle. The people then spread the Tent of Meeting over the tabernacle.

After that, Moses placed the ark in its designated place in the Holy of holies and put the tables of the covenant in the ark. The lamp stand was positioned near the ark. He filled the cups with olive oil and lit the lamps to burn from evening to morning every day as the Lord had commanded:

It shall be a due from the Israelites for all time throughout the ages.

Exodus 27:21

When Moses had finished the work, the cloud covered the Tent of Meeting, and the Presence of the Lord filled the tabernacle...When the cloud lifted the Israelites would set out on their various journeys; but if the cloud did not lift they would not set out. For over the tabernacle a cloud of the Lord rested by day, and fire would appear in it by night, in the view of Israel throughout their journeys.

Exodus 40:34–38

The cloud over the tabernacle is understood as a reminder of the cloud that covered Sinai, the presence of which would be with them wherever they traveled. The "fire... in it by night" might have been a reminder to kindle the lamp stand, but I choose to think of it metaphorically as the same fire in the bones to be avoided on the Sabbath—the fire of the creativity and enthusiasm that built the tabernacle.

The repetitions of 25-31 and 35-40 reveal the importance of this matter to the writers. Little did they know, the day would come when their words would present a field day for existential interpretation.

The monumental task facing Moses was the modification of a culture. As has been said before, taking the people out of Egypt was easier than taking Egypt out of the people. As anticipated on Sinai and necessitated by the calf incident, a strategic plan was being implemented.

Assman observed, "The most efficient way of erasing a memory is by superimposing it on a counter memory. To make a people forget an idolatrous rite is to put another rite in its place."[4] Moses' strategy was to replace rites and cults practiced for the sake of idols with practices glorifying the Invisible, by appealing to the people's senses.

Moses began his instructions with a reminder that no matter how important the mission, keeping the Sabbath would always take precedence. He added a new fillip by fusing the religious and social elements into a guide for adapting the Sabbath to everyday life. He was again stressing the importance of the holiness of time.

Following the exhortation to keep the Sabbath, Moses asked for gifts to the Lord and volunteers to work on the tabernacle. The idea that they were now a free people was given further credence by the making of gifts and the providing of labor as options, unlike the life of mandatory servitude they had known. Of their own free will, they could make a difference and so achieve a feeling of self esteem.

In effect, they were now physically and emotionally freed from the existential failure of four hundred years of slavery in Egypt.

The Torah has two terms for the sanctuary, the tabernacle and the tent of meeting. Together, they express the dual functions of a place for the presence of the invisible God and a place for God and Moses to communicate. To make the idea of its holiness more concrete, God gave the following instruction that would have been familiar to the people: "You shall take the anointing oil and anoint the tabernacle and all that is in it to consecrate it and all its furnishings, so that it shall be Holy" (Exodus 40:9).

Since the tabernacle would be integrated with observance of the Sabbath, the two aspects of the original idea of the Holy, the separation of time (the Sabbath) and space (the tabernacle) were now conjoined. This was a notable step in Moses' goal of uniting God's presence with the conception of Holiness.

Moses' objective was to introduce into the tabernacle setting artifacts and practices familiar to the people yet not defiling of the commandment "You shall not make for yourself a sculptured image." The first step was an appeal to the olfactory sense because the nose knows.

Of all the human senses, that of smell heads the list in evoking memories. Whenever I sense the aroma of baking bread, I recall going with my mother to the bakery on Westminster Street in Detroit to buy *challa* (egg bread) for Shabbat. The scent of Lilac-Veget lotion evokes an immediate image of my grandfather shaving. In the same context, aromatic experiences from childhood are with all of us.

The Israelites were no different in this respect. When the tabernacle was filled with the aromas of incense, burnt offerings, or anointing oil, they would readily identify them as "soothing savors before the Lord." Surely, Moses had matched these scents with those he knew as a young lad in Egypt.

Living in ancient Egypt, the people could not escape the influence of the sun deity, Aton-Re. There was an abundance of hieroglyphics representing worship of the sun long before Ikhnaton formulated a religion based on worshiping the sun's rays. It followed that a source of light would be central to convey the presence of God in the tabernacle.

Moses and Bezalel went all out to create an exquisitely designed and ornamented lamp stand, later known as a *menorah*. There were cups for burning oil at the top of the central shaft and at the ends of three branches from each side, seven in all.

The light of the menorah burned from evening to morning and was known as the *ner tamid* (the regular light) because of the designated fixed routine that attended its lighting. It seems strange that no significance was given to the idea that each lamp represented a day of the week, the predominate one the Sabbath. Reference to this came later.

Other furnishings were an altar for burnt offerings, an altar for incense, a table for bread offerings, a laver for the priests to wash their hands and feet and an elegant veil in front of the arc. The tabernacle and its furnishings were the epitome of elegance and splendor. Little wonder, the designers knew what they were doing; Moses grew up amidst the quintessence of splendor, and Bezalel honed his skills fabricating similar objects for Egyptian royalty.

One need only to consider the ingenuity of placing the ark in the geometric center of that section of the tabernacle designated the Holy of holies. The only item that was not familiar to the people was the ark of the covenant, which was placed in the most important location. Moses understood what retailers now call "positioning." The polarization of the old and the new brought the relevance of the ark and its contents into sharp focus.

Most amazing of all is how these objects have stood the test of time. The ark has remained the central figure in synagogues throughout the ages, usually containing several Torah scrolls upon which the five books of Moses are inscribed. They are usually clothed in covers, crowns, and breastplates fashioned after the priestly vestments. Consistency has not been lost.

Arks, more often than not vertical in stature, continue to house the commandments embodied in the Torah. Renderings symbolizing the stone tablets appear elsewhere at the discretion of the architects.

An exceptional design stands in Temple Israel, West Bloomfield, Michigan. It is an adaptation of the portable ark described in Exodus 25:10. In keeping with the biblical description, it has simulated carrying poles and cover. For convenience, the opening is on the side which faces the congregation.

Forgive a play on words, but I often ask children, "How did the menorah get its name?" Answer: It was originally called the lamp stand. The first time the cups were filled with oil and set ablaze the people stood back in awe, overcome by the splendor before them and exclaimed, "*Mah norah* (How awesome)!" That's not a *midrash*; I made it up.

But it could be true. The menorah designed by Bezalel was a beautiful work of art and when lighted would have filled the tabernacle with a warm glow, which, when reflected from the gold and silver furnishings, must have been breathtaking. Replications adorn most houses of Jewish worship today.

The menorah, flanked by two olive branches, is the national emblem of the State of Israel. It has been found in stone relief on the floors and walls of ancient synagogues as well as on the Arch of Titus in Rome.

No longer does it burn from sunset to sunrise. That function has been superseded by a perpetual light (*ner tamid*) that burns continuously in the synagogue, symbolizing the continuous presence of God.

Artists love the opportunity to create unique designs for perpetual lights with their personal touches. My first choice for such effective creativity hangs in the sanctuary of Congregation Shaarey Zedek, Southfield, Michigan. It replicates the burning bush casting a warm, orange glow through bush-like branches, triggering memories of the encounter.

Further evidence of Moses' genius is shown by his achievement of symbols to create perceptions of YHVH's presence in relation to the Holy. Even moderns, to a great extent, need the objective to embrace the subjective. But if icons were—and still are—effective, what about the tabernacle itself, the objectivity of an enclosure?

The sum total of the tabernacle and its furnishing was designed to engender an overall effect of spiritual awe. However, of singular importance was the activity that took place there. It was within the tabernacle that the Eternal was said to have resided, and it was there he spoke to Moses. It was also central to Sabbath worship.

When we visit the majestic gothic cathedrals of Europe, whatever our religious persuasions, we are uplifted by the soaring grandeur of the architecture. Even an atheist would have a hotspot on "the orientation association area of the brain." In simple terms, many visitors participate in mystical experiences.

Apart from the architecture is the human history that comes to mind when reflecting upon those whose life cycle events took place within such walls; people coming in penitence, joy and sorrow; baptisms, weddings, and funerals; thousands upon thousand of worshipers over the centuries.

When we visit the ancient synagogues of Europe, though they are less imposing architecturally, while beautifully designed, their walls resonate with centuries of prayer and emotion. In Germany, we experience the added emotions surrounding Crystalnacht and those who were cruelly escorted away before their allotted times. In both situations, we experience the holiness of space and time.

My congregational home, Temple Beth El in Bloomfield Hills, Michigan, is interesting in the present context. Architect Minoru Yamasaki expressed his feelings for history and contemporary style by replicating, on a grand scale, the Tent of Meeting in a modern idiom.

The sanctuary, elliptical at its base, soars to a height of seventy feet above the congregation, which is bathed in light from a skylight and surrounding, peripheral windows. The virtual tent hangs from a central truss flowing outward to simulate the appearance of fabric.

The ark of polished brass, a practical substitute for pure gold, tall, and elegantly slender, is reminiscent of the tablets. To complete the symbolism, the doors are embossed with the traditional Hebrew numerals of the commandments. A brass menorah placed on one side of the ark is illuminated with wax candles on appropriate occasions, and a simple brass perpetual lamp is suspended from the ceiling by a thread-like cord.

Behind the ark, a screen converging to the apogee of the structure symbolizes the screen over the ark in the tabernacle. And yet the screen is unlimited in its potential impressions. It creates the illusion of soaring upward forever, lifting the spirits of the congregation complimented by the glorious sounds of the organ pipes, which it conceals. Simplicity replaced the ornate with no loss of sensitivity.

We must pause to question why there is such concern with edifices and furnishings in the modern age. Few continue to believe God dwells only in the sanctuary. Religious people often affirm that God dwells everywhere or only in the human mind. Nevertheless, beautiful surroundings, links with history, and the presence of others of like mind connect us with the spirituality of the moment when the presence of God seems to fill the sanctuary.

Symbols are wonderful as long as we respect Heschel's admonishment, "Not to have a symbol, but to be a symbol."[5]

Yamasaki created the awesome feeling of a cathedral with the spirit of the tabernacle. Entering at the rear and proceeding down the long aisle to the *bima* (platform) with the choir singing and surrounded by the congregation, I have often experienced an existential rush—a flood of memories of the people who made a difference in my life giving rise to my authentic self.

Zornberg sees a thread of polarity woven throughout the tapestry of the Exodus. It is the theme of opposing poles such as the arrogance of Pharaoh against the humility of Moses or the ecstatic experience of crossing the sea versus the dissonance of the desert.

However, poles can either attract or repel. In the building of the original tabernacle, we have seen how Moses fused the polarities of objectivity and subjectivity to reinforce each other by employing objective symbols that relate to the senses to enhance the subjective perception of the Invisible.

Rabbi Nahum Sarna cogently expressed in his Torah commentary a concise description of the Grand Narrative: "The Book of Exodus, which opened with a tale of misery and oppression, closes on an auspicious note. Israel is assured that day and night, the Divine Spirit hovers over it, guiding and controlling its destiny."[6] The journey has not ended; in fact this is only the beginning. With additional preparation the journey from slavery to freedom is about to take place.

Oh that I might dwell in Your tent forever.

Psalm 61:5

Exterior view of Temple Beth El, today. Sanctuary designed by Minoru Yamasaki symbolizing The Tent of Meeting.

Interior view of Temple Beth El, today. Showing the
contemporary adaptations of the Mishkan (tabernacle)
open Ark with Torahs, Manorah, Ner Tamid, and Hebrew
letters symbolizing the commandments on the Ark doors.

Ner Tamid
(perpetual light from two former TBE sanctuaries).

Carved mahogany Ark from two former TBE sanctuaries.

MORAL GRANDEUR

After the regression of the calf, the zeal with which the Israelites constructed the tabernacle and its appurtenances was a step in the right direction. To maintain that momentum, the next step was to introduce the functions of the *mishkan* (tabernacle) and the priests by beginning with activities the people could relate to—rituals, customs, ordinances, and punishments they could comprehend.

Having set forth a body of law Moses apparently resolved that laws would not be sufficient to effect proper behavior; it would be necessary to extend the idea reflected in the tenth commandment, "Thou shall not covet...," voluntary ethical behavior. The people would need personal virtues to make life worthwhile for themselves and the community. They needed to create a sense of personal authenticity.

These would involve two disparate faces of God. The first face was the one Rabbi Heschel called "moral grandeur" is associated with sacrifices, ordination of the priests, ethical values, and days of celebration. The other face relates to punishments and retributions. The present chapter deals with moral grandeur emphasizing ethical living; the other face of God will be the subject of the following chapter.

The first words of Leviticus follow on the heels of those that conclude Exodus and maintain the compelling flow of the Grand Narrative. They begin with the instructions to the Israelites of how to attain the status of "a kingdom of priests and a Holy Nation"[1] (Exodus 19).

> The Lord called to Moses and spoke to him from the Tent of Meeting, saying: Speak to the Israelite people, and say to them: When any of you presents an offering of cattle to the Lord, he shall choose his offering from the herd or from the flock.
>
> If his offering is a burnt offering from the herd, he shall make his offering a male without blemish… The priest shall turn the whole into smoke on the altar as a burnt offering, an odor pleasing to the Lord.
>
> Leviticus 1:1–6

Reading these opening verses, my thoughts were the questions David might have asked had this been his Bar Mitzvah portion.

His first would be the obvious, "What are burnt offerings?" The second might have been related to what he learned in religious school: "Are not the sacrifices we make to God sacrifices of the heart?"

Sometimes, I think children were born to challenge our ideas and make us think. Even when they're not with us, we've become conditioned to anticipate their questions.

To the first question, I would have replied that such offerings to deities were as old as ancient man and known to have been practiced by the Egyptians. Certain sacrificial animals were completely consumed by flames and were called burnt offerings. It was thought the smoke ascended to appease whatever the deity; in this case "a pleasing odor to the Lord."

However, there were two significant differences between biblical sacrifices and those of ancient Egypt. There were no human sacrifices, such as those of defeated warriors as practiced in Egypt.[2] Further, the sacrifices were accessible to all the people rather than a select few, such as kings and priests.

To the second question, I would have replied that David's religious teacher was expressing a concept from a later biblical period, beautifully articulated by the prophet Amos:

> If you offer Me burnt offerings I will not accept them;
> But let justice well up like water,
> Righteousness like an unfailing stream.
>
> Amos 5:22–24

It is conveyed in the words of a song we sing in services following the silent devotion:

> May the words of my mouth and the meditations of my heart be acceptable in Thy sight, O Lord, my rock and my redeemer.
>
> Psalm 19:15

To understand Leviticus, we must consider the text in its historical perspective. It was directed to the Israelites only one year removed from Pharaoh's taskmasters and, even more recently, from their antics surrounding the calf. It begins with procedures for making animal and bread sacrifices to the one and only God.

Indeed, the emphasis of Leviticus in Amos's words is *justice* and *righteousness*, but they are conveyed in a unique way with holiness being characterized as separation. It was a theme that germinated in the hot sand at the bush, grew at Sinai, and blossomed from the fertile ideological soil of Leviticus as a sense of supernatural Presence.

Many times, justice and righteousness are presented in contexts of separation. Typical are clean and unclean, sacred and profane, good and evil, chaos and order. However, more insightful ideas of separation in broader areas of human thought and history are:

- ❑ Experience and tradition
- ❑ Egyptian paganism and Mosaic monotheism
- ❑ Existence and essence

God encouraged the Israelites to emulate him and in trying to be more like him to achieve a modicum of holiness. "You shall be Holy, for I, the Lord your God, am Holy" (Leviticus 19:2). The intent is to inspire the Israelites to choose a better way of life separate from the merely mundane.

As Sartre expressed it three thousand years later, "Before you come alive, life is nothing: it's up to you to give it a meaning, and its value is nothing else but the meaning you choose."[3] That which is the very heart and center of existentialism is the absolute character of the free commitment by which every man realizes himself.

Moses' problem arose because he was dealing with a throng of riffraff—people coming from a culture in which tolerance and submission were the keys to survival. Would they be capable of making existential choices leading to self-fulfillment? Aware that cultural change would be more difficult than the escape from Egypt, Moses—not the most patient of men—was committed to the task he chose to make happen.

He began with an easy one—sacrificial rites that the people understood. Nehama Leibowitz expanded on the idea: "The Hebrew word for sacrifice, *korban*, is derived from a root meaning 'to draw near,' implying that a sacrifice is but a method given to us by God for drawing near to Him. In other words, it does not allude to an automatic process set in motion by the bringing of an offering, but is a conscious effort on the part of the worshipper to propitiate his Creator."[4]

In Leviticus chapter 5, we begin reading about crimes and punishments—legal infractions of two kinds, those against God and those against humankind. The following are sins against God:

> If a person incurs guilt:
>   When he has heard a public imprecation and.....he does not give information....
>   Or when a person touches any unclean thing....
>   Or when he touches human uncleanness....

Or when a person utters an oath to bad or good purpose...but later finds himself culpable....

When he realizes his guilt in any of these matters, he shall confess that wherein he has sinned.

Leviticus 5:1–5

Interestingly, the text goes on to say the punishment shall be a sheep or a goat, but if a person's means do not suffice, a lesser offering will do. A descending scale of the offender's various offerings is suggested, ending with an "epha of choice flour." Thus, modification of punishment applies to sins committed against God.

The following relates to sins against an individual:

The Lord spoke to Moses, saying: "When a person sins and commits a trespass against the Lord by dealing deceitfully with his fellow in the matter of a deposit or a pledge, or through robbery, or by defrauding... When one has thus sinned and, realizing his guilt... He shall repay the principle amount and add a fifth part to it. He shall pay it to its owner."

Leviticus 5:20–24

In addition, he must give the priest a ram or equivalent as a guilt offering. The priest will then make expiation on his part. Clearly, the Lord is more concerned with the wrong done by one person to another than with offenses against him alone.

Had David been asked what he remembered about Leviticus, the chances are he would have referred to the laws about keeping kosher—separating foods designated as fit (kosher) for human consumption from those that were not to be eaten.

> The Lord spoke to Moses and Aaron, saying to them: "Speak to the Israelite people thus: 'These are the creatures that you may eat from among all the land animals.'"
>
> Leviticus 11:1

David would not be alone. To this day, the dietary laws are of cardinal importance in many Jewish homes. Most Orthodox Jews adhere somewhat closely to these rules because they are "written." Less rigorous adherents believe the practice of abstinence was meant to make a person stronger; others take it as a way of maintaining their Jewish identity.

Whatever, a case can be made for the proscription of certain foods as a precaution arising from Moses' Egyptian experience—those foods not served at Pharaoh's table. He chose to not let the people take a chance on foods he himself had not safely eaten.

Abstinence from pork has more adherents than any other of the forbidden foods. The biblical rationale might have originated from the bad history of the pig in ancient Egypt or possibly the economic consideration that pigs eat the same foods as humankind.

To encourage eating right, God chose the carrot, not the stick. Such persuasion was expressed in one of the most elegant utterances in the history of language.

> For I the Lord am your God: you shall sanctify yourselves and be Holy, for I am Holy. You shall not make yourselves unclean through any swarming thing that moves upon the earth. For I the Lord am He who brought you up from the land of Egypt to be your God: you shall be Holy, for I am Holy.
>
> Leviticus 11:44–46

One must not get the idea that God was like a Jewish mother telling her children what not to eat. In contrast to Pharaoh who ruled with an iron hand, he was a loving, nurturing God who preferred that his people lift themselves up, sanctify themselves, by making free, constructive choices.

However, when we encounter these words again in Leviticus 19:2, they will be presented in a much broader perspective. They will convey not only what not to eat, but the choice of elevation over diminishment—the elevation of sanctification by ethical conduct. The existential potential of these words is at once apparent, but at this point, we see no more than the tip of the iceberg.

Yet, even here, the awesomeness of the phrase "you shall be Holy for I am Holy" triggers a mystical experience, a feeling of transcendence. It's like losing oneself in one of Beethoven's last piano sonatas or in the faces in Rembrandt portraits.

Composed when he was stone deaf and suffering a prolonged and painful dying of cirrhosis, opuses 109 to 111 reflect Beethoven's soul, his inner being, the recapitulation of his life, the anguish of his later years amalgamated with the pure joy of music.

Looking into the eyes in a Rembrandt portrait, we sense a mirror of the soul—an elderly man with tragic failings and sufferings or the tender emotions of a young girl having just stopped crying.

It seems those gifted with artistic genius ascend higher and lower on the emotional scale than the rest of us; they reach higher levels of elation and lower extremes of despondency. One need only consider Leonard Bernstein, one of the truly great geniuses of the twentieth century. To him, his failure to compose anything like a Mahler symphony was tragic in contrast to his euphoria in conveying the joy of music to young people.

The laws of purity and impurity regarding food have relevance because, in one form or another, they exist in current practice. In an existential sense, choosing between pure and impure foods may be synonymous with making the choice between pure and impure thoughts and actions.

The verses that follow are of largely academic interest because they're related to life in the desert three thousand years ago. They deal with the responsibility for matters of disease and cleanliness that were delegated to the priests.

For example, the priests had to determine whether a skin affliction was a rash, a discoloration, or leprosy. If a leprous lesion appeared to heal, a priest had to determine if the cure was permanent. If some sort of fungus growth appeared in a person's dwelling or on a garment, the priest would be called to supply a remedy.

Defilement through childbirth is dealt with at length. The new mother was treated as ritually unclean until a period of purification took place following which a lamb was brought to the priest for a burnt offering. The role of the priest in all such matters was ritualistic; he was not responsible for playing doctor.

These passages are anything but edifying reading. However, our sages were able to put a positive fillip on them. "They pointed out that man was not given a perfect world, but one which needed improving and demanded the exercise of man's own creative abilities."[5] While somewhat contrived, Leibowitz has proposed a neat perception.

There was similar thinking regarding circumcision. The words "On the eighth day he shall be circumcised (Leviticus 12:3)" led Rabbi Akiva to opine, "Circumcision signified a perfecting (Hebrew, *tikun*) of the natural endowments of man, the attainment of a moral, spiritual state transcending that already given him."[6]

With a little ingenuity, it's possible to put a positive spin on archaic customs to create perceptions to make them relevant in a contemporary context.

Throughout the preceding chapters, taken in their entirety, we see much repetition. The phrases "The Lord spoke to Moses" and "I the Lord am your God" appear a number of times. Through such repetition, Moses was doing his best to make it undeniably and abundantly clear that the message was God's and not his.

The Torah portion beginning at Leviticus 19:1 is traditionally known by the first key-word, *kedoshim*, "Holiness." Moses' idea of the transcendent concept of Holiness, in contrast to the mechanical aspects of time and space, comes to fruition, *Kadosh.* (Holy) gradually came to indicate not the physical separation of God and man but the spiritual gap between human inadequacy and Divine perfection.[7]

Holiness is extended to virtually every area of life: family, calendar, business, civil and criminal law, social relationships, and sexuality. Most of the laws deal with the ethics of interpersonal relationships. As such, they represent the essence of ethical monotheism.

Heschel introduces the subject this way: "The awareness of divine dignity must determine even man's relationship to his own self... Indeed, Jewish piety may be expressed in the form of a supreme imperative: 'Treat yourself as an image of God.' It is in the light of this imperative that we can understand the meaning of the astonishing commandment."[8]

> The Lord spoke to Moses, saying: "Speak to the whole Israelite community and say to them: 'You shall be Holy, for I, the Lord your God, am Holy.'"
>
> Leviticus 19:1–3

The second line sounds like something we've heard before, but there's a difference. The words "You shall be Holy" are to be addressed to everyone—not only

Moses, not only the priests, not any select few, but *to the whole Israelite community*. The Jew believes this to be true for all humankind from that moment on.

"We have here a series of noble rulings appealing to man to show kindness to the weak, respect for the aged, refrain from bearing a grudge, avoidance of oppression and robbery. These are fundamental laws demanding a high standard of moral conduct, calling on man to imitate the attributes of God."[9]

"You shall be Holy, for I, the Lord your God, am Holy" is a gracious, unconditional expression of love. It is far removed from the kind of love we see in *Sex and the City* or *Desperate Housewives*, often called falling in love or infatuation or just simple lust.

It is love, as Erich Fromm—an eminent existential psychologist—explained, that gives life to the emotional and intellectual potentialities of humankind, gives birth to the authentic self. Fromm's idea of love implies care and responsibility for life, for the growth and development of all human powers and is clearly an act of will.[10]

The commandment is addressed to the entire community, but the focus is on the individual. Each must discover the secret of imitating the attributes of God for himself or herself, achieving a modicum of holiness each in their own way.

David Hermelin, whose contributions to the greater Detroit community were many and far reaching, conveyed this idea of self-determination in his approach to fund raising, "Give until it feels good." Feeling good about it is the return of ethical living.

Hermelin personified what Sartre generalized as the ultimate goal of Jewish ethical living: "The Jew thinks that the end of the world, of this world, and the upsurge of the other will result in the appearance of the ethical existence of men who live for one another."[11]

My grandfather was fond of saying, "Virtue is its own reward." The reward of ethical living is ethical living, nothing more. "Holy shall you be"—practice ethical living and through enriching your own life become a blessing to the community.

"Holy shall you be" casts a new light on the enigmatic words in Genesis, "And God said, 'Let us make man in our image, after our likeness.'" "Holy shall you be"—four words symbolizing God's creation of humankind capable of divine imitation.

Heschel speaks of it as the exaltation of man: "In this exalted world man's position is unique. God has instilled in him something of Himself... Likeness to God is the essence of man. Man's privilege is, as it were, to augment the divine in the world."[12]

In another context, he stated it in existential terms, "Israel's reply to Moses, *We will do and we will hear*, was interpreted to mean, 'In doing we see.' By enacting the spiritual on the stage of life we perceive our kinship with the divine. Our acts, then, are waves that flow toward the shore of God."[13]

> The Lord spoke to Moses, saying: "Speak to the whole Israelite community and say to them:
> 'You shall be Holy, for I the Lord, your God, am Holy.

'You shall each revere his mother and his
father, and keep My Sabbaths:
'I, the Lord, am your God.'"

Leviticus 19:3

In one brief statement introducing the subject of
ethics, three of the commandments are referred to.
Why these in particular? Because in matters of ethics,
relationships matter. Connections with the lofty images
of God emerge from Sabbath observance; interactions
with parents, whose lips utter the basic dos and don'ts of
social harmony become the roots of human solidarity.

The closing words "I, the Lord, am your God" echo
the first and paramount commandment, reinforcing
the idea of the God of Israel being the promulgator
of the laws and commandments. The phrase, in several
variations, is rendered thirteen times in Leviticus,
numerically equal to the number of the attributes
of God.

"You shall not insult the deaf, or place a stumbling
block before the blind. You shall fear your God"
(Leviticus 19:14). The eloquence of the writers is a
constant source of amazement, of which this exquisite
metaphor is another example. We can only wonder
in amazement how they knew how to express their
thoughts so eloquently.

Taken literally, the admonitions are pointless. Only
an extremely perverse person would be so callous
in relating to the handicapped. In a broader sense,
the implications are directed to misleading those
who are deaf or blind in particular situations, not

to take advantage of incompetence or treat others contemptuously. Or, on occasion, to disabuse someone of creating a self-imposed stumbling block for even wealth can be a stumbling block if not used wisely.

But why the disquieting admonition "You shall fear your God"?

Bamburger offers a contemporary example, "One who has sold worthless stock to a widow could argue, 'I really believed it was valuable and that I was helping her to get rich.' Who could prove he or she was insincere? Therefore, adds *Sifra*, wherever the law is something 'entrusted to the heart,' the Torah cautions, 'You shall fear[1] your God.' He, alone knows what your motives were."[14]

"Love your neighbor as yourself: I am the Lord" (Leviticus 19:18).

In the words of Rabbi Akiva, "*Love your neighbor as yourself* is the major principle of the Torah."[15]

The idea of loving one's fellow man becomes clear when we think of love in Fromm's terms of love that nurtures self-realization and gives rise to the development of human potential of love that conveys respect and avoids domination or possessiveness.

Such love comes from one who has acquired self-love through practicing the art of ethical living, knowing what it is to feel good about one's own self, and being comfortable with one's self image. Clearly,

---

[1] The Hebrew word *yara* translated here as "fear," also has the meaning "revere," as used above in "revere his mother and father."

the words are meant to imply a process in the same way that striving to become one's authentic self is a process.

An obvious question intrudes into our elevated train of thought. How could the Israelites, only one step removed from the existential failure of slavery, relate to the idea of loving one another? What's more the elusive idea of loving a stranger in their midst?

More than a thousand years later, Hillel, one of the greatest rabbis of his age, asked himself the same question and so rephrased the commandment in the negative, "What is hateful unto you, don't do unto your neighbor."[16] This formulation constitutes a useful interpretation, especially since Hillel was more concerned with a particular window in time than with existential validity. Erich Fromm had not yet appeared upon the scene.

For polarized contemporary views, one can compare those of Freud and Heschel. Freud asked the question as to how one could love his neighbor who probably wasn't worth it.

Heschel opined that the Torah calls upon us to love not only the virtuous and wise, but also the vicious and stupid.

To Freud, I would respond, "Who am I to make such a call?" To Heschel, my admired mentor, I would humbly inquire, "When we reach out to our neighbor and he does not extend his hand, rather than persist, might we better seek another neighbor?"

The theme becomes even more compelling when we read:

> The stranger who resides with you shall be to
> you as one of your citizens; you shall love him
> as yourself, for you were strangers in the land of
> Egypt: I, the Lord, am your God.
>
> Leviticus 19:34–35

Thirty-six times in Exodus, we are reminded to have concern for the stranger.

These words expand the previous command, beyond that of a fellow Israelite, to embrace even strangers, assimilating them as members of the community. It goes beyond the injunction, discussed in Exodus to "remember" the stranger. In the context of primitive society where every stranger was considered an enemy, it is quite relevant.

Cynthia Ozick elegantly sets forth the concept of loving the stranger:

> "Love thy neighbor as thyself" is a glorious, civilizing, unifying sentence, an exhortation of consummate beauty.... It reveals at once the little seed of parable: the phrase "as thyself." But we are still with our neighbor. We are still, with the self, in psychology. The more compelling sentence carries us there—and you will hear in it history as metaphor.[17]

I can think of no more fitting words to conclude our discussion of the *Holiness Code* than those of the great Rabbi Solomon B. Freehof:

> The perfect Holiness of God is beyond our reach. We know that we can never attain it. Yet

it can affect our lives, for we strive towards it. That is what the Bible means when it says, *Ye shall be Holy; for I, the Lord your God, am Holy.*

Having established a body of laws prescribing ethical behavior and more laws about sexual offenses and laws concerning the priests, Leviticus enters a new phase in taking up days of celebration—times of renewal.

> The Lord spoke to Moses, saying: "Speak to the Israelite people and say to them: 'These are my fixed times, the fixed times of the Lord, which you shall proclaim as sacred occasions.
>
> On six days work may be done, but on the seventh day there shall be a Sabbath of complete rest, a sacred occasion. You shall do no work; it shall be a Sabbath of the Lord throughout your settlements. These are the set times of the Lord, the sacred occasions, which you shall celebrate.'"

Leviticus 23:1–3

So reads the introduction to a description of what we now call the holidays. With respect to the individual celebrations, they appear as limited sketches of our contemporary observances. In general, they simulated agricultural festivals of the time with one important new twist; they were to be celebrated by all the people, not merely the priests and dignitaries as practiced elsewhere.

What are we to make of these words? Their brevity opens the door to interpretation, and since in biblical parlance, repetition is the key to relevance, several perceptions emerge:

❑ The optimism of defined time
❑ The predominant position of the *Shabbat*
❑ A nexus linking *Shabbat* and the holidays

The optimism of defined time was not that new to Israel; it was already realized in their life style with the weekly observance of Shabbat. In Egypt, every day was like the next—a day of drudgery followed by another day of drudgery with nothing to break the monotony. Shabbat changed all that.

Now, something new had been presented with the holidays separating one agricultural season from another as a *sacred occasion, which you shall celebrate.* Work would never be the same. In addition to Shabbat, the Israelites would also know days when they could rest and express thanks to God communally.

At the beginning of the spring season, on the fourteenth day of the first month, they were to celebrate the grain harvest conjoined with remembering how God redeemed them from Pharaoh's domination. It was to be called *Pesach* (Passover) because on that day God ordained that the angel of death would "pass over" the houses of the Israelites. The holiday was to last seven days, during which time unleavened bread (and no leavened bread) was to be eaten to remind the celebrants of the hasty departure from Egypt.

The Torah teaches that every Jew must relive the Exodus in order to feel as if they personally participated in the departure from Egypt. To implement the instruction there are numerous reminders in all Jewish religious observances. The story of the Exodus is not a segment of the past, but it has been kept alive as the Grand Narrative of the Jewish people.

The holiday, known today as *Shavuot* (Weeks), occurred fifty days later to celebrate the gathering of the harvest planted at the time of Passover. The third harvest festival, now called *Succoth* (Booths), completed the cycle of harvest festivals—spring, summer, and fall were all dignified by days of complete rest. The biblical description of *Shavuot* concludes with an ethical enjoinder applicable to all harvests, another opportunity to give until it feels good.

> And when you reap the harvest of your land, you shall not reap to the edges of your field, or gather the gleanings; you shall leave them for the poor and the stranger: I am the Lord, your God.
>
> Leviticus 23:22

No opportunity was lost to proclaim the importance and sanctity of the Sabbath. The idea of complete rest might easily have become an end in itself had Moses not been constrained to consistently remind the people that it was not only a day off but, primarily, *a sacred occasion.*

It does not suffice to say the Shabbat is preeminent over the days of celebration because it was ordained as a commandment. More so, as Heschel tells us, "In the Ten Commandments the term Holy is applied to one word only, the Sabbath."[18]

The connection of holidays to Shabbat is revealed in the way that agricultural celebrations of the period, which had been around for a long time, were retrofitted to conform to the observance of Shabbat. They were changed to include everyone and mandated complete rest for all.

It must come as a disappointment to contemporary Jews when they see the minimal descriptions of the days they know as the High Holy Days. In the present context, *Rosh Hashanah* and *Yom Kippur* are not mentioned by name. *Rosh Hashanah* (New Year's Day) was designated as the first day of the seventh month.

> You shall observe complete rest, a sacred occasion, a reminder by [horn-] blasting, a proclamation of Holiness[20]
>
> Leviticus 23:24

Despite their brevity, these few words capture the essence of the holiday—a day of rejoicing in YHVH and a day of remembrance.

Yom Kippur (The Day of Atonement) was discussed earlier in Exodus 16 and was given more attention than Rosh Hashanah. And in Leviticus we read:

> Mark the tenth day of this seventh month is the Day of Atonement. It shall be a sacred occasion for you: you shall practice self-denial and you shall bring an offering by fire to the Lord, you shall do no work throughout the day, for it is a

Day of Atonement on which expiation is made on your behalf before the Lord.

Leviticus 23:27–28

For a better understanding of the phrase "expiation is made on your behalf," we refer to Leviticus 16 and Deuteronomy 29–30. The former discusses how the priest sacrificed burnt offerings for the people so they would be cleansed before the Lord "to make atonement for all the Israelites for all their sins once a year."

Rather than the priests making atonement, Deuteronomy puts it in personal terms within the reach of the individual, each one within the limits of his or her potential:

> Surely, this instruction which I enjoin upon you this day is not too baffling for you, nor is it beyond your reach. It is not in the heavens... Neither is it beyond the sea... No, the thing is very close to you, in your mouth and in your heart, to observe it.

Deuteronomy 30:11–14

The Reform High Holy Day Prayer Book *Gates of Repentance* converts this thought into a personal confession: "You do not ask me, 'Why have you not been great as Moses?' You do ask me, 'Why have you not been yourself? Why have you not been true to the best in you?'"[20]

> Mark on the fifteenth day of the seventh month, when you have gathered in the yield of

your land, you shall observe the festival of the Lord Succoth to last seven days. On the first day you shall take the product of hadar trees, branches of palm trees, boughs of leafy trees, and willows of the brook, and you shall rejoice before the Lord your God seven days.

Leviticus 23:39–40

So Moses declared to the Israelites the set times of the Lord.

Leviticus 23:44

In conjunction with Passover, *Shavuot* is the second act in the drama of reliving the Grand Narrative. *Succoth*, which comes six months after Passover, recalls the wanderings of the Israelites after vacating Egypt and acknowledges gratitude to God for the fall harvest.

From the succession of three fall holidays, celebrations that follow in such close succession as to be considered as one, an important pattern emerges. *Rosh Hashanah* was a proclamation of God's Holiness, *Yom Kippur* centered on pleas to God for forgiveness of sins against Him, and *Succoth* characterized God's response to the prayers and supplications of the preceding holidays with a harvest—a harvest from the land and a harvest of the spirit expressing God's forgiveness of sins committed against Him.

This pattern became the format for the Shabbat service. The opening portion of each service features the glorification of God followed by petitions to God. God responds with words read from the Torah; thus, words spoken three thousand years ago come to fruition as the response to contemporary prayers, thereby glorifying Jewish services of worship.

When we move ahead to Leviticus 25:1, we read of the plans for inhabiting the Promised Land. Word of reaching the destination served a dual purpose: it reminded the Israelites that the land flowing with milk and honey was not out of sight and sketched a legal framework for a new life there.

> When you enter the land that I assign you, the land shall observe a Sabbath of the Lord. Six years you may sow your field and six years you may prune your vineyard and gather in its yield. But in the seventh year the land shall have a Sabbath of complete rest, a Sabbath of the Lord: you shall not sow your field or prune your vineyard.
>
> Leviticus 25:2–4

God then decreed the fiftieth year to be a jubilee year: "You shall hallow the fiftieth year. *You shall proclaim liberty throughout the land* [emphasis mine] for all its inhabitants" (Leviticus 25:10).

The emphasis calls attention that these words are inscribed on the Liberty Bell, which announced the signing of the Declaration of Independence and resonate throughout our Constitution of the United States of America.

There follow several verses relating to care for the impoverished and enslaved. On the fiftieth (jubilee) year, slaves were to be given their freedom, loans and debts cancelled, and interest on loans negated. The wealthy were admonished to realize that their wealth and their lands were blessings from the Lord.

Moses anticipated the self-perpetuating tendencies of wealth and poverty. "The land must not be sold beyond reclaim, for the land is Mine; you are but strangers, resident with Me" (Leviticus 25:23).

The people are admonished to create a just society and to revere the Lord. In this way, they would achieve the holiness as commanded by God.

Heschel articulated moral grandeur and, more importantly, practiced it. He marched in the forefront and went to jail with Martin Luther King. His actions gave credence to his words from, The Biblical View of Reality: "In doing we experience grandeur."[21]

THE OTHER FACE OF
GOD IN LEVITICUS

S everal passages were omitted from the previous
chapter because of their incompatibility with
the tenor of moral grandeur. While the ideas on
such matters as animal sacrifices, skin eruptions, and
childbirth defilement permitted a positive spin, casting
the cases that follow in a positive light is a far greater
challenge. One must now contend with the treatment
proposed for the blasphemer.

> And the Lord spoke to Moses, saying, "Take
> the blasphemer outside the camp; and let
> all who were within hearing lay their hands
> upon his head, and let the whole community
> stone him. And to the Israelite people speak
> thus: 'Anyone who blasphemes his God shall
> bear his guilt; if he also pronounces the name
> Lord, he shall be put to death. The whole
> community shall stone him; stranger or
> citizen, if he thus pronounced the Name, he
> shall be put to death.'"
>
> Leviticus 24:13–17

This is strong if not disturbing stuff. It greatly exceeds "an eye for an eye" (Exodus 20:24).

"If anyone maims his fellow, as he has done so shall it be done to him: fracture for fracture, eye for eye, tooth for tooth. The injury he inflicted on another shall be inflicted on him" (Leviticus 24:19–20).

The above, which refers specifically to injuries to a fellow human, is generally interpreted to mean the punishment shall not exceed the crime. What then is to be said about the punishment to the blasphemer? You will recall from an earlier passage (Leviticus 5:1–24) sins against another human were considered more flagrant than those committed against God.

In the above, "stone him, stranger or citizen," are words in conflict with the commandments to love your neighbor and the stranger. Such treatment of the blasphemer is so inconsistent with the tenor of Leviticus that one must pause to wonder who was uttering such harsh invectives. Was it really Moses articulating the words of God, or was he improvising?

The answer is found in the thirteen attributes of God in Exodus 34:8–9: "A God showing mercy (*rachamim*) and favor, slow to anger, abundant in steadfast love (*chesed*) to the thousandth generation, forgiving iniquity, transgression and sin."

In the above as we have seen, the Hebrew word *chesed* is frequently used in the Bible to describe the relationship of God to humankind. Rabbi Nelson Glueck made a convincing argument that *chesed* conveys the meaning of constancy, steadfast love, steadfast reliability. Glueck commented: "It is but a short step from *chesed* to *rachamim*: *chesed* is covenantal loyalty; *rachamim* is forgiving love."[1] This is understood as the essence of God.[2]

As we read further, the discontinuity becomes magnified. The next passage begins on a compassionate note:

> If you follow My laws and faithfully observe My commandments, I will grant rains in their season, so that the earth shall yield its produce and the trees of the field their fruit... I will grant you peace, and you shall lie down untroubled by anyone... I will be ever present in your midst: I will be your God, and you shall be my people.
>
> Leviticus 26:3–12

God is strongly advising the people that the choice is theirs. "If you observe My commandment I will be ever present in your midst." The people were largely in control of their own destiny.

But the asymmetric sound of discordance quickly follows:

> But if you do not obey Me and do not observe all these commandments... I will wreak misery upon you—consumption and fever, which cause the eyes to pine and the body to languish, you shall sow your seed to no purpose, for your enemies shall eat it...
>
> And if for all that, you do not obey me, I will go on to discipline you sevenfold for your sins, and I will break your proud glory... I will bring a sword against you to wreak vengeance for the

covenant, and if you withdraw into your cities,
I will send pestilence among you, and you shall
be delivered into enemy hands.

Leviticus 26:14–25

The specifics of threats and retributions continue
at great length, and are clearly inconsistent with the
positive motivation of the carrot not the stick, reward
not punishment, and "I will be your God, and you shall
be my people."

God's voice not only has a different tone, but implies
a different speaker. It is certainly not the voice heard in
Exodus 19:5, "If you will obey Me faithfully and keep
my covenant, you shall be My treasured possession."
Instead, we have the intimidation of dire punishments
virtually negating any freedom of choice other than
fear of the consequences.

Taken in context of some three thousand years
ago, it would have gotten attention because it would
likely have been perceived as the voice of God with
the familiar overtones of Pharaoh. With generations
of exposure to autocracy, the Israelites would not have
questioned its authority. However, a modern perception,
not conditioned by life in the tar pits, subjects it to
greater scrutiny.

It is reasonable to assume that Moses, who knew
his audience well, took certain liberties of authorship
to prevent a recurrence similar to that of the calf. More
importantly, it would be beyond reason to believe that
God, after encouraging the people to aspire to holiness,
would have been the source of such reproachful

language. It would require a leap of faith of which I am not capable.

How then are we to understand the words "the Lord called to Moses, and spoke to him"? The existential validity is in the eye of the beholder, but the focus of the eye can be sharpened by the thoughts of great minds that have pondered the question.

Rosenzweig offers an interpretation of inspiration, "What man hears in his heart as his own human speech is the very word which comes out of God's mouth."[3]

Mozart said much the same thing, without attribution to a divine source, when he said, "Whence and how my ideas come I know not; nor can I force them."[4] However, Salieri—a God-fearing soul in Peter Schaffer's play *Amadeus*—declared, "God needed Mozart to let Himself into the world."[5]

It's likely Peter Schaffer put words into the mouth of Salieri paraphrasing George Bernard Shaw's encomium of Mozart. His score of *The Magic Flute* is "the only music that would not sound out of place in the mouth of God." Ironically, the opera was inspired by Mozart's adulation of the principles of freemasonry.

Will and Ariel Durant thought in terms of imagination: "Moses ruled bloodlessly by inventing interviews with God."[6]

In Kabbalistic imagery, the mapping of the world yields six compass points, the four directions, up and down, and a seventh point representing the heart of the matter. It is the hidden meaning, the truth that cannot be translated into words. The elusive origin of God's voice is symbolized by the seventh point.[7]

From Heschel, we have an applicable rabbinic comment: "The statement, 'God's word came to me,' was employed by the prophet as a figure of speech, as a poetic image…. He turns revelation into dialogue"[8]

These ideas will hopefully strike matches in the dark to illuminate the elusive presence of God in dialogue with man. In the army, we were taught that in combat one was to never light three matches in succession, so doing might enable the enemy to locate, aim, and fire. In this case, it is unlikely the striking of several matches might be harmful. Rather, an abundance of matches struck may help light the way.

Buber had this in mind when he said, "Readers are able to confirm the truth of biblical passages through their own existential experience and should only accept as truth whatever in the text corresponds to that experience."[9]

While Moses may have acted out of his own compulsion as a response to the idea of a God whose desire was for the people to lift themselves up and freely commit to self realization, he knew that to accomplish the task he would have to bend the rules a little.

Between the lines, we perceive that Moses was concerned with the very difficult goals of establishing motivation and control. To achieve these objectives he spun the ideas of fear rather than hope; fear being a more effective emotional stimulator. If Moses conveyed the impression that God spoke out of both sides of his mouth, it was his own conscious decision. Moses was dedicated to turning the mixed multitude into a great nation.

Although I was initially tempted to add a question mark to the chapter title, "The Other Face of God in Leviticus?" it would have been disconcerting. God had many faces, as expressed by the phrase, "I will cause all of My goodness to pass before you," but playing the multifaceted stern taskmaster was not one of them. It was Moses, and not God, who wished to appear as "*this teetering bulb of dread and dream.*"[10]

SCENES SEEN THROUGH THE PRISM

The Israelites were about to pack their bags, disassemble the *mishkan* (tabernacle), and venture into the wilderness on their way to the Promised Land. Before rejoining them, there is a narrative section of Leviticus that will be enlightening, chapters 8, 9, and 10.

AARON'S SONS

The rabbis taught there is no early or late in the Bible. Since there is no hierarchy among passages, there is no need to visit them in order. Now that we have considered Moses' liberties with authorship, we will be able to see what took place in a new light.

The scene is at the grand opening of the Tent of Meeting. Unlike the present custom of a show opening on the road, the formal opening of the tabernacle occurred at Sinai and involved the enactment of the ceremonies described in Exodus chapter 29.

The stage was the tabernacle and the cast featured Moses, Aaron, and Aaron's sons, for God had decreed in Exodus chapter 28 that Aaron's four sons would be priests and Aaron the high priest. All the Israelites were in attendance. The drama featured the initiation of formal worship with the altar being used for the first time.

> The Lord spoke to Moses, saying: "Take Aaron along with his sons, and the vestments, the anointing oil, the bull of sin offering, the two rams, and the basket of unleavened bread; and assemble the whole community at the entrance of the Tent of Meeting."
>
> Leviticus 8:1–3

Moses washed Aaron and his sons with water and dressed them with the prescribed clothing and adornments of the priesthood. He consecrated Aaron, the tabernacle, and all its appurtenances with anointing oil. The bull and the rams were ceremoniously slaughtered and certain of their parts turned into smoke on the altar "for a pleasing odor, an offering by fire to the Lord."

The ordination of Aaron and his sons took place over seven days, during which time they were not permitted to go outside the entrance. In keeping with the customs of the time, numerous sacrifices were made for which there were fires inside and out.

"And Aaron and his sons did all the things that the Lord had commanded through Moses" (Leviticus 8:36).

The ceremonies continued on the eighth day with more sacrifices and offerings as Moses commanded. Then Moses and Aaron came out from inside the Tent of Meeting.

They blessed the people, and the Presence of the Lord appeared to all the people. Fire came forth from before the Lord and consumed the burnt offering and the fat parts on the altar. And all the people saw, and shouted, and fell on their faces.

Leviticus 9:23–24

Now Aaron's sons Nadab and Abihu each took his fire pan, put fire in it, and laid incense on it; and they brought near before the Lord outside fire, such as He had not commanded them. And fire came forth from the Lord and consumed them; and so they died at the instance of the Lord. Then Moses said to Aaron, "This is what the Lord meant when He said: 'Through those near to Me I show Myself Holy, And gain glory before all the people.'" And Aaron was silent.

Leviticus 10:1–3

In other words, what Moses said was that God would not forgive a flaw or error in anyone he chose to fill an important office even if, as in this case, the offense was not clearly stated. The apparent inconsistency is that God had already forgiven Aaron for his complicity in the calf incident by appointing him high priest.

The obscure accidental deaths of Nadab and Abihu have given rise to much speculation because they were both neophytes just learning to be priests with no ritualistic or ceremonial experience. What their crime was has also puzzled commentators who have debated the issue over the years. Before we look at this episode through the existential prism, let's review what scholars have said.

- ❑ Many assume that Nadab and Abihu were a little tipsy from too much wine, which was prohibited to priests while on duty.
- ❑ Some have said it was an accident, but it underscored the need for priests to perform rituals precisely according to the rules.
- ❑ Others accuse them of having peeked behind the screen to observe the presence of God, which was definitely forbidden.
- ❑ A fourth school of thought proposes they did not sin, but they died a holy death and ascended to heaven.

My choice is none of the above, for I cannot relate to a God Who would deliberately take the lives of Aaron's sons for a sin committed against the Lord. Let's scratch our heads and try to find a more plausible explanation.

Considering their lack of experience in performing the approved rites and the inherent dangers with handling fire, it was probably a terrible accident and at most a misdemeanor. Why, then, did Moses attribute their punishment to the will of a compassionate God, punishment for an act much less grievous than worshiping the calf?

The Israelites had just witnessed a horrendous accident. They were people who had been conditioned by Moses to perceive acts of radical amazement as attributed to the invisible God who was capable of working wonders. Here, in the presence of God, Moses thought the people were likely to question why God had not intervened to avert such a calamity. They had also learned from their Egyptian experience that deities were supposed to do such things.

Moses reacted impulsively by announcing that God had acted in retribution. The people had just seen what happened to those close to God who performed inappropriately. What, then, might happen to them if they were disobedient?

Improvisation is common when less important irregularities occur on stage. It's not unusual for a phone to ring at the wrong time or fail to ring at the appropriate time. Then, an actor has to improvise. The story is told of John Barrymore who missed an entrance. When the actress on stage called out, "Where in the world are you?" He replied, from off-stage so all could hear, "Terribly sorry, darling, I'm having trouble with my zipper."

Moses ingeniously improvised on the spot to keep the Israelites from losing faith by making one of the all-time great AD libs. Despite the demise of his nephews—a traumatic experience for him—he stayed in character to provide a convincing explanation, which was followed by the prompt removal of their bodies. We have previously learned Moses would set the script aside to realize his mission. This was no exception.

The reason to visit the final chapters of Leviticus before the tragedy that befell Nadab and Abihu should be apparent. We had to first see a pattern of inconsistencies to accept the fact that Moses could resort to being disingenuous about what he saw as a higher duty imposed by God. In the death of his nephews, we can feel his anxiety at having to mislead the Israelites in order to better lead them.

THE PRIESTLY BLESSING

Now we turn the Torah scroll to the book of Numbers. The name Numbers comes from the beginning verses, which deal extensively with taking a census of those who could bear arms and to properly arrange the tribes in marching order. The Hebrew name, *B'midbar* (in the wilderness) is more appropriate. It aptly describes the desert they had to traverse to reach the Promised Land.

It began on the first day of the thirteenth month following their departure from Egypt. In addition to census taking, legal and sacramental issues were discussed and camp was broken.

The Israelites had lived in the shadow of Sinai for almost a year. The prospect of venturing into the unknown, removed from God's presence, must have been disquieting. Then they heard a familiar voice— that of Moses intoning the words of God—which was the same assuring voice that had told them, "You shall be Holy, for I, the Lord your God, am Holy."

The message, known to Jews and Christians everywhere as the priestly blessing, is a literary gem of singular beauty. At a moment of fear of the unknown and separation from Sinai, Moses presented stirring words of reassurance:

The Lord spoke to Moses: "Speak to Aaron and his sons: Thus shall you bless the people of Israel. Say to them:

'The Lord bless you and protect you!

'The Lord deal kindly and graciously with you!

'The Lord cause His Presence to be felt by you and grant you peace!'

So are they to put My Name upon the children of Israel, that I may bless them."

Numbers 6:22-27

We have Rabbi Norman Roman to thank for this insightful translation. His interpretative version beautifully conveys the message meant for the Israelites and for the current Judaic-Christian generation as well. However, the rhythm of the Hebrew language and its linguistic patterns are lost in translation. The three blessings were presented in a succession as three, five, and seven words, spreading them out as they ascend in greater importance:

Y'varech'cha Adonai v'yishm'recha!
Ya'er Adonai panav elecha veechuneka!
Yisa Adonai panav elecha v'yasem lecha shalom!

It is also important to remember that the poem is couched in the singular, whereas the English pronoun *you* is ambiguous. Even though delivered by the priests to the community at large, the listeners were to perceive the blessings as directed to them individually.

The words following the blessing are also instructive. From whatever circumstance, the Israelites were to recognize the blessing spoken by the priests as the words of the Lord. "So are they to put My Name upon the children of Israel, that I may bless them" conveys the message that the priests are but an instrument for the outpouring of God's graciousness upon humankind.

While in a figurative sense we shall accompany the Israelites from the comfort of an armchair and the advantage of historical hindsight, we can gain a perspective of what they will encounter through the poetic eye of Chaim Potok:

> They traveled as donkey nomads through a great and terrible wilderness of rugged mountains, crossing valleys bounded by immense granite cliffs. Often the floor of a valley would be littered with stones and boulders torn loose from the hills by winter rain and washed down by torrents that formed sudden rivers rushing with enormous energy through the crevices, gouging the hills and gullying the earth of the valleys.
>
> It was late summer when they set out. A dry relentless heat burned up the days. The sun carved the landscape into geometrical patterns of light and shade. The nights were chilling. There was little water.[1]

MURMURING AND GRUMBLING

Knowing how Moses thought and his awareness of what Potok described, it's reasonable to assume Moses frequently extolled the wonders of the Promised Land. Such encomiums might have whetted the appetites of the Israelites until they experienced the "great and terrible wilderness." Their disdain and discomfort were made clear by their reactions after leaving the mountain:

> The people took to complaining bitterly before the Lord. The Lord heard and was incensed; a fire of the Lord broke out against them, ravaging the outskirts of the camp.
>
> Numbers 11:1

> If only we had meat to eat. We remember the fish that we used to eat free in Egypt. We remember the cucumbers, the melons, the leeks, the onions, and the garlic. Now our gullets are shriveled. There is nothing at all! There is nothing but manna to look to!
>
> Numbers 11:4–6

> Moses heard the people weeping, every clan apart, each person at the entrance to the tent. The Lord was very angry and Moses was distressed.
>
> Numbers 11:10–12

They became suspicious and resentful of Moses. Two men, Eldad and Meded, acted the prophet in the camp. When Joshua implored Moses to restrain them, Moses responded in words reflecting his inherent humility and compassion: "Are you wrought up on my account? Would that all the Lord's people were prophets, that the Lord put His spirit upon them. (Numbers 11:29).

His sister and brother, Miriam and Aaron, complained to the Lord that Moses' wife was an Ethiopian woman. They said, "Has the Lord spoken only through Moses? Has He not spoken through us as well" (Numbers 12:2).

> The Lord came down... and He said to Aaron and Miriam, "Pray hear my words: If a prophet of the Lord should arise among you, I would make Myself known to him in a vision. I would speak to him in a dream. Not so with my servant Moses; he is trusted in all My house. With him I speak mouth to mouth, plainly and not in riddles, and he beholds the likeness of the Lord. How then did you not shrink from speaking against My servant Moses?"
>
> Numbers 12:5–8

Did the Lord speak to Miriam and Aaron? We wonder how words of the God that inhabited the mind of Moses might have migrated into the heads of his brother and sister.

Perhaps through sustained personal contact with their inspired brother, something like osmosis took place.

Rabbi Morris Adler offered a clarification: "There is no condition, no circumstance, and no travail in which people cannot hear the voice of God if they are determined to hear it."[2]

Buber explains in his book *Moses* that Numbers consists of fragmented incidents to tell of the wanderings of the people and bring out the character of Moses. By whatever means these words came to Aaron and Miriam, they speak volumes about their brother Moses. "Prophets have visions which must first be interpreted. But to Moses *from mouth to mouth* the word is blown into the man, as from a breath it inspires itself into him."[3]

So Near and Yet So Far

In its characteristic brevity, the Bible cites but a few of the expressions of malcontent. Considering the adverse conditions, these would have been accompanied by many more, which typified the murmurings and grumblings. Moses accepted various minor uprisings as symptoms of the rebellious nature of the riffraff. As a result, they succeeded in reaching *Kadesh-barnea* at the Southern tip of Canaan, the promised land.

From his previous sojourns, Moses was familiar with the territory and its inhabitants. He knew the people would not be welcomed with open arms; occupation could only be achieved by a forceful intervention. From his military training as an Egyptian, he had learned the first step was reconnaissance. He also understood that those who would perform such dangerous work would be more receptive if they understood the directive as coming from the Lord.

> The Lord spoke to Moses, saying, "Send men to scout the land of Canaan, which I am giving to the Israelite people, send one man from each of their ancestral tribes, each one a chieftain

among them." So Moses, by the Lord's command, sent them out from the wilderness of Paran.

Numbers 13:1–3

When Moses sent them to scout the land of Canaan, he said to them, "Go up into the Negev and on into the hill country, and see what kind of country it is. Are the people who dwell in it strong or weak… and take pains to bring back some of the fruit of the land."

Numbers 13:17–20

These scouts returned after forty days, reported to Moses, Aaron, and the whole community, and showed them the fruit of the land. The following was their report:

> We came to the land you sent us to, it does indeed flow with milk and honey, and this is its fruit. However, the people who inhabit the country are powerful, and the cities are fortified and very large….
>
> Caleb [one of the scouts] hushed the people before Moses and said, "Let us by all means go up, and we shall gain possession of it, for we shall surely overcome it."
>
> But the men who had gone up with him said, "We cannot attack that people, for it is stronger than we." Thus they spread calumnies among the Israelites about the land they had scouted. "The country that we traversed and scouted is one that devours its settlers. All the

people that we saw in it are men of great size...
and we looked like grasshoppers to ourselves,
and so we must have looked to them."

Numbers 14:27–33

The existential reality of *panim* (faces) is manifest
in the observations of the twelve spies. They saw what
they expected to, or wanted to, both in themselves and
their adversaries.

The whole community broke into loud cries,
and the people wept that night. All the Israelites
railed against Moses and Aaron. "If only we
had died in the land of Egypt... or if only we
might die in this wilderness! Why is the Lord
taking us to the land to fall by the sword? ... Let
us head back for Egypt."

Then Moses and Aaron fell on their faces
before the assembled congregation. And Joshua
and Caleb, who had scouted the land, rent their
clothes and exhorted the Israelites, "The land
we traversed and scouted is an exceedingly
good land. If the Lord is pleased with us, He
will bring us into that land, a land that flows
with milk and honey, and give it to us; only you
must not rebel against the Lord. Have no fear
of the people of the country for the Lord is
with us." As the whole community threatened
to pelt them with stones, the presence of the
Lord appeared in the Tent of Meeting to all the
Israelites.

And the Lord said to Moses, "How long
will this people spurn Me, and how long will

they have no faith in Me despite all the signs
I have performed in their midst? I will strike
them with pestilence and disown them."

Numbers 14:1–12

After repeating these harsh words to the people,
Moses proceeded to plead with God to show mercy.
God acquiesced. Instead of *pestilence and disownment*,
God decreed that those over the age of twenty were
to wander in the wilderness for forty years. A new
generation would then inhabit the land the others
had rejected.

What the scouts reported to Moses told more about
the scouts than it told about the territory. Ten scouts
felt like grasshoppers compared to the inhabitants
while the other two were not intimidated. Ten had
not shaken their slave mentality; two had exhibited
authentic maturity. All twelve saw what their experience
had conditioned them to see, and so they conveyed
opinions, not facts.

Joshua and Caleb submitted their minority report,
which led to a fierce eruption of fear and doubt from
the populace regarding the possibility of conquering the
land. Moses was thereby convinced of the impossibility
of culture change when culture shock was so dominant.
Visions conditioned by life in slavery had prevailed
once more.

Moses had selected the elite among the people,
the leaders of the twelve tribes. Why did so many
of them express such fear? Had they forgotten how
they prevailed against the Amalekites a year earlier?

However, in the battle against the Amalekites, Moses had been close at hand like a cheerleader. In this situation, they were alone; each scout acted on his own for forty days. The ten obstructionists seemed to have visualized the alleged giants as though they were Pharaoh's taskmasters.

In the face of a potential mutiny, Moses had to call on the words of God to quell an insurrection. Following stern words from the Lord, Moses prayed for and affected a judicious compromise. The Israelites were to wander in the desert until the generation which left Egypt had died out. With the exception of Caleb and Joshua, those who would inhabit the Promised Land would be a new generation, not infected by the mentality of slavery.

Viewed through the existential prism, there is a noteworthy message in the above. These few verses clearly elucidate the difficulty of culture change. Here was a body of people with a huge opportunity for a better quality of life, but anticipated change could not be accomplished in less time than a generation.

Thinking about what can be learned from this segment of biblical history recalls the difficulty the United States had instilling culture change in Iraq. A persuasive lesson might have been learned from Numbers 14:1–12. George Santayana remarked in *The Life of Reason*, "Those who cannot remember the past are doomed to repeat it."[4]

What does culture change have to do with existentialism? Is it not a societal issue? Sartre would argue that the whole is equal to the sum of its parts—society is a body made up of individuals. Thus the Israelites as a group were not in an existential sense ready until the individuals, or at least most of them, became their authentic selves by embodying the new mentality conceived in freedom.

This whole sequence clearly defines something we've seen several times before. Moses had an amazing understanding of both the psychology of individual behavior and the dynamics of group action.

KORAH

Shortly after the spy incident, Moses and Aaron encountered an unholy controversy. The rabbis tell us the following anecdote was an amalgamation of four insurrections merged into one. They refer to it as Korah's rebellion.

> Now Korah, along with Dathan and Abiram, together with two hundred fifty Israelites... betook themselves to rise up against Moses... They combined against Moses and Aaron and said to them, "You have gone too far! For all the community are Holy, all of them, and the Lord is in their midst. Why then do you raise yourselves above the Lord's congregation?"

The rebels clearly misinterpreted the words "Holy you shall be for I the Lord your God am Holy." Korah based his revolution on the false assumption that God's words implied all were Holy. Therefore, by what arrogance was Moses telling the people what is right and what is wrong? In Korah's mistaken logic, all the people were already Holy; therefore, commandments were no longer necessary.

The fallacy was twofold. Korah confused leadership with conditions of righteousness, and he took the position that "Holy you shall be" is a given rather than an enjoinder to become holy.

Buber called attention to two earlier statements of Moses referring to all Israel as Holy; one was in the form of a commandment, the other an aspiration. "This contradiction... converts the words of Moses into their opposite, changing request and hope into insolent self-assertion."[5]

Upon hearing the rebel's impertinent accusation, Moses fell on his face, presumably in prayer. He then rose and told Korah that in the morning "the Lord will make known who is His and who is Holy." Dathan and Abiram then interceded on behalf of the malcontents: "Is it not enough that you brought us from a land flowing with milk and honey to have us die in the wilderness, that you would also lord over us" (Numbers 16:13).

The action reached an unfortunate culmination. Moses called the antagonists out of their tents and announced that if they die of an unheard of cause, it was done by the Lord who sent Moses to do all these things because they have spurned the Lord.

> Scarcely had he finished speaking when the ground under them burst asunder, and the earth opened its mouth and swallowed them up... They went down alive into Sheol [the

underworld] with all that belonged to them;
the earth closed over them and they vanished
from the midst of the assembly. All Israel
around them fled at their shrieks, for they said,
"The earth might swallow us."

Numbers 16:31–38

Korah's rebellion portrays the Israelites' discontent
at being deprived of entry into the Promised Land and
condemned by God to struggle in the wilderness. Their
threat of insurrection was punished by a mass burial of
the insurgents whose fate was meant to strike the fear of
God into any who still might harbor similar intentions.

Under the circumstances, Moses apparently used an
earthquake, presumably a natural disaster, to maintain
order. The story should only be taken in that context.
If not, it would convey the disturbing idea that God
rewards good and punishes evil—an argument used
throughout the ages for persecution of the Jewish
people. As we learned from Leviticus, virtue is its own
reward, nothing more, and fear of the consequences is
not consistent with the pursuit of Holiness.

A further case in point is that of Miriam and Aaron
who contested the authority of Moses. Miriam was
punished with a white skin eruption common in the
desert. It appeared to be leprosy, but it healed in seven
days. Aaron, on the other hand, was not punished
physically, but the rabbis tell us that he suffered pangs
of remorse. Of the two, the self-inflicted punishment
of Aaron was clearly more onerous and consistent with
the pursuit of Holiness as expressed in Leviticus.

THE GENIUS OF LEADERSHIP

We pick up the story thirty-eight years later. The Israelites had returned to Kadesh- barnea, and Miriam died soon after their arrival. They were then only two years away from the deferred opportunity to enter the Promised Land, but despite the arrival of a new generation, the Israelites continued their accustomed petulance and grumbling. Moses knew there was no time to vacillate.

> The community was without water, and they joined against Moses and Aaron. The people quarreled with Moses, saying "If only we had perished when our brothers perished at the instance of the Lord! Why have you brought the Lord's congregation into this wilderness for us and our beasts to die there? Why did you make us leave Egypt to bring us to this wretched place, a place with no grain, or figs or vines or pomegranates? There is not even water to drink!"
>
> Moses and Aaron came away from the congregation to the entrance of the Tent of Meeting, and fell on their faces. The Presence of the Lord appeared to them, and the Lord spoke to Moses, saying, "You and your brother Aaron take the rod and assemble the community, and before their very eyes order the rock to yield its water. Thus you shall produce water for them from the rock and provide drink for the congregation and their beasts."
>
> Moses took the rod from before the Lord, as He had commanded him. Moses and Aaron

assembled the congregation in front of the rock; and he said to them. "Listen you rebels, shall we get water for you out of this rock?" And Moses raised his hand and struck the rock twice with the rod. Out came copious water, and the community and the beasts drank.

But the Lord said to Moses and Aaron, "Because you did not trust Me enough to affirm My sanctity in the sight of the people, therefore you shall not lead this congregation into the land I have given them."

Numbers 20:2–12

This extended text again underscores the rebelliousness of the people, the stern decree of the Lord, and the impatience of Moses, and now, we confront an obvious dilemma.

Everett Fox asks a pertinent question: "Why exactly Moses and Aaron received such a terrible punishment for a moment of indiscretion will not go away. Can it really be that the towering figure of Moses, liberator and lawgiver, parent and prophet, is to be done away with in the blink of an eye over a justifiable temper?"[6]

Fox is not alone in questioning the conventional wisdom. The opinions of the rabbis and sages on this issue are various and often sound somewhat contrived:

❑ Leaders in the Bible must be beyond reproach.
❑ Moses and Aaron did not trust God enough to affirm His sanctity.
❑ Moses addressed God's people in anger, "Listen, you rebels!"

❑ They were being punished for the previous crimes of the calf and the spies.

Through our existential prism, we may see this controversy in a new light. Moses was willing to color God's words to avoid jeopardizing the likelihood of the Israelites obtaining their goal.

In this case, Moses saw the writing on the wall, especially since he was approaching his one hundred and twentieth year. His eyesight had dimmed, his strength had ebbed, and his energy had diminished. He knew he was no longer capable of leading Israel to the Promised Land. The same was true of Aaron, several years his senior. It was time for Joshua, his appointed successor, to take over.

Having been God's emissary and having led the people through the sea to Sinai and throughout the wilderness, it might have fomented an insurrection if he were to summarily discard his mantle of leadership. Moses, therefore, created the ruse that it was God's punishment that he was not allowed to remain their leader because of his intemperate behavior unbecoming to God's emissary. Moses chose to sacrifice his personal goal of entering the land for the more likely success of the grand vision of Israel becoming a holy people.

Consider the corollary. Had he passionately thought it was his mission to lead the people across the Jordan and word had come to him from God that he was forbidden to do so, he might have chosen not to reveal the message and proceed accordingly. It wouldn't have been the first time Moses would have acted of his own volition.

In light of this interpretation of his conduct, it is useful to reflect on a familiar prior anecdote. Having seen through the prism how Moses might have skewed his words to achieve a higher purpose, consider these lines from the calf incident:

> Moses stood up in the gate of the camp and said, "Whoever is for the Lord, come here!" And all the Levites rallied to him. He said to them, "Thus says the Lord, the God of Israel: Each of you put sword on thigh, go back and forth from gate to gate throughout the camp, and slay brother, neighbor and kin."
>
> Exodus 32:26–27

In this matter as well, Moses did not follow through. He did not pursue the dictates of the Lord to *slay brother, neighbor, and kin* and, curiously, chose not to slay his own brother, Aaron. Moses was clearly prone to contradicting God's words when he felt the occasion justified doing otherwise.

> You can rely on the support of others in your action, which obviously has certain limits because you're not going to live forever.[7]
>
> —Sartre

CHOOSE LIFE THAT YOU MAY LIVE

These are the words that Moses addressed to all Israel on the other side [east] of the Jordan.

Deuteronomy 1:1

The transition is almost seamless. The juxtaposition of Numbers and Deuteronomy admits of no apparent lapse of time. However, there is a dramatic change of style and spirit as we open the new book.

To better capture the tenor of the text that follows, we need to think of the excerpt above as a paraphrase of Exodus 1:8: "These are the words that Moses addressed to the generation of Israel that knew not Sinai."

Moses had abdicated his desire to enter the land, either by choice or fiat. There was limited time remaining to imbue the new generation with the culture he unsuccessfully endeavored to create for and imbue in their mothers and fathers.

He had led this new generation and their progenitors from Egypt to Sinai and through the rigorous wilderness to where he was standing within proximity of the Promised Land. During that time, he had done his best to help them draw perceptions of the Invisible from their own lives, but even forty years was not enough.

Now, in Deuteronomy, known in Hebrew as *Devarim* (Words), Moses—not known to be a man of words—suddenly finds his voice. He addressed Israel in a series of three discourses, clothed in moving eloquence, to convey the existential messages their mothers and fathers had failed to fully grasp.

The new style casts Moses speaking in the first person singular, delivering God's message without the familiar refrain, "The Lord spoke to Moses, saying, 'Speak to the children of Israel and say to them.'" He was delivering final words of encouragement and admonition for success and well being in a strange land.

Rabbi Freehof describes the "beautiful generosity of spirit, this humaneness and kindliness, so characteristic of the Book of Deuteronomy... The sentences flow into each other 'til all the duties of man to fellow man are exalted to the grandeur of man's love to an ever-loving God."[1]

In Moses' new voice, we find a confluence of communal and individual responsibility, repetition of laws, and exhortations to live, and not just to exist. The existential ideas that were often hidden between the lines earlier become readily apparent in Deuteronomy.

Freedom of choice is almost blown out of proportion. Several times, Moses voices concern that the people will choose to ignore the commandments once they have become settled in the new life style across the Jordan. One might think he saw them as Sartre saw

Adam and Eve: "Perhaps Adam had never thought of eating the fruit of the tree of knowledge. But once God forbids it, he knows that he can do it; ergo, he is free to do it, and does."[2]

The idea that reality is in the eye of the beholder has became more compromised because it was now the generation once removed for whom the Exodus had not been experienced first hand. Moses spoke to the children of those who exited Egypt as if they themselves had been there. "You remember when you were slaves in Egypt." He hoped they would be capable of projecting what their forbears experienced as having happened to them.

His point was well conceived but not easily conveyed, for it lacked the effectiveness of actuality. Experience can become knowledge only if it can be conceptualized. On the other hand, Moses made a convincing argument that *mitzvoth* are instruments by which Holiness is experienced.

Deuteronomy is virtually an existential primer, and its first principle that man is nothing but what he makes of himself flows through Moses' discourses. Sartre argued, "Subjectivism means, on the one hand, that an individual chooses and makes himself, and, on the other, that it is impossible for man to transcend human subjectivity."[3]

> It was in the fortieth year, on the first day of the eleventh month, that Moses spoke to the children of Israel according to the instructions the Lord had given him.
>
> Deuteronomy 1:3

To explain the alleged decree that God forbade him to cross the Jordan, Moses offered these thoughts to the people:

> I pleaded with the Lord at that time, saying, "O Lord God, You who let Your servant see the works of Your greatness, and Your mighty hand, You whose powerful deeds no God in heaven or earth can equal! Let me, I pray, cross over and see the good land on the other side of the Jordan, that good hill country, and the Lebanon." But the Lord was wrathful with me on your account and would not listen to me.
>
> Deuteronomy 3:23–26

Now, two years later, it was their fault; previously it was his fanaticism. He wanted them to understand God's words the way he, Moses, desired them to be perceived.

Moses' newly found literary eloquence gets progressively better. Here's his argument to the people on becoming a great nation:

> For what great nation is there that has a God so close at hand as the Lord our God whenever we call upon Him? Or what great nation has laws and rules as perfect as all this instruction that I set before you this day?
>
> But take utmost care and watch yourselves scrupulously, so that you do not forget the things that you saw with your own eyes and so that they do not fade from your mind as long

as you live. And make them known to your children and your children's children.

Deuteronomy 4:7–10

And because He loved your fathers, He chose their offspring after them.

Deuteronomy 4:37

Moses was speaking to the generation that followed those who saw it with their own eyes. It's as if they saw it through the stories they heard. His amazing ingenuity was to conjoin what they had to see through the eyes of their fathers with the obligation to transmit the message to future generations. Moses' words had to be remembered and taught from generation to generation: "If you search there for the Lord your God, you will find Him, if only you seek Him with all your heart and soul" (Deuteronomy 4:29).

Where is *there?* Moses anticipated that without his being *there* they could not see the land through his eyes. They might go through life with blinders on. In the land where water flowed in great abundance, who would remind them that if it weren't for God they wouldn't be *there?* They would still be in Egypt, and water from a rock would not have been an option.

If we take the word *there* in a general sense, we will have discovered one of the profound subtleties in the Bible. Buber waxed especially eloquent in consolidating these thoughts: "Moses made use of everything potentially visible in nature, every kind of natural existence, for His manifestation."[4]

He taught them to grasp through their senses what was hidden from their minds. There would be little miracles happening every day—a baby's smile, a beautiful flower, a rainbow, the good feeling of doing a *mitzvah*. Buber called such happenings "thought moments."

Moses recalled his own mystical experience on Sinai and knew that if they sought God with *heart and soul*, they would surely find him. "If you hallow this life you meet the living God."[5] Moses intuitively understood what Newberg discerned from brain scans.

The appearances of radical amazements, thought to be miracles, had to be sought, taught, and reinforced. The separation of the sea would have been taken as a fortuitous happening had Moses not been there to make known that it was an act of the Lord. In his words to the people, Moses had conveyed the art of conditioned perception.

The first discourse of Deuteronomy is essentially a history lesson for the new generation of Israel, relating the forty-year journey from Egypt to the Jordan. He spoke of the wonders the Lord worked on behalf of their progenitors to enhance their amazement of God.

Having emphasized selected highlights, we turn to the second discourse in which Moses defined the covenant God had made with their fathers, the laws of Exodus, Leviticus, and more to create a homogeneous society.

The Ten Commandments were repeated with slight but significant modifications of the fourth. It opens with the words, "Observe the Sabbath day and keep it

Holy," while in Exodus it is written as, "Remember the Sabbath day and keep it Holy."

The difference is subtle but significant. It suggests that forty years earlier, the idea was something new and different, not to be forgotten. Further, they were to remember when there was no Sabbath, no day of rest. After forty years, the Sabbath had become a fait accompli.

But Moses had not forgotten the word *remember*; he employed it in a different context by adding the phrase: "Remember that you were a slave in the land of Egypt and the Lord, your God, freed you from there with a mighty hand and an outstretched arm; therefore, the Lord, your God, has commanded you to observe the Sabbath day" (Deuteronomy 5:15).

Remember that you were a slave. Because had you been there, you would have been a slave. The amazing foresight of this directive is that it has been passed along from parent to child, generation after generation, to this day.

We can only intellectualize what it might have been like to be slaves in Egypt. Fortunately, our memory banks don't provide a lot of clues as to what it would be like to bake bricks under a hot desert sun. But we are able to connect to three thousand years of history as metaphor, which can be passed along to our children.

Plaut offers an interesting insight: "In Exodus 20, the fourth commandment makes the Sabbath day Israel's sanctified time… Even as God renews daily the work of creation, so Israel renews weekly its awareness and appreciation of the ongoing process.

"In Deuteronomy, on the other hand, the Sabbath is founded, not only on the sanctification of time, but also on the historic creation of God's chosen people from the mire of slavery, and thus the day is humanized and its humanization is extended to all members of Israel's society."[6] Moses' new formulation extends the Sabbath to include focus on self and others.

Following the modified commandments, Moses again presents words from the Lord: "And the Lord said to me, 'May they always be of such mind to revere Me and follow all My commandments, that it may go well with them and with their children forever'" (Deuteronomy 5:26).

The question immediately comes to mind as to why Moses needed the higher authority of God to make this statement about freedom of choice? Could it not have effectively come from his lips in the first person?

The answer resides in the guilt cast by the final fillip, "that it may go well with them." In other words, if they do not choose to revere God and follow His commandments for their own sake, they should do it for their children. This compelling argument, when spoken by God, represents a Hobson's choice—an option that offers no alternative. It resonates with God's words preceding the Ten Utterances at Sinai: "if you will hearken to My voice and keep My covenant, you shall be My special treasure from among all peoples" (Exodus 19:5).

Rabbi Henry Slonimsky, dean of the Jewish Institute of Religion, explained, "In truth, choseness is far more than love, it is ineluctable destiny: the individual Jew may drop away, but Israel as a whole is held inexorably fast." [7]

Plaut sees this verse as "the proof text for the doctrine of human free will. God is hoping that Israel would always revere Him and follow His commandments. This obviously implies that God does not know whether or not Israel will do His will, for Israel, like all humanity, is free to obey or not to obey." [8]

How inspiring that Moses coined a phrase that would live on for more than three thousand years—presumably forever. Moses tried to capture in words the perceptions he hoped had been conveyed by the experiences of forty years, little knowing these eight Hebrew words would take on a life of their own:

> *Shema Yisrael! YHVH Elohenu, YHVH Echad!*
> *Hear, O Israel! The Lord is our God, the Lord alone!*

Deuteronomy 6:4

Just to say that the words live on diminishes their significance. They are the first Hebrew words learned by most Jewish children, and the last words uttered by religious (and some not so religious) Jews. Generally known as "The Watchword of the Faith," to every Jew, they have unique associations and meanings.

According to Rabbi Gunther Plaut, "The *Shema* holds a position of importance in Jewish practice unparalleled by any other verse. It is recited in religious services, on retiring at night and dramatized at the conclusion of the Yom Kippur service, where it is followed by the sevenfold exclamation, 'The Lord is God.'"[9]

The phrase is spoken of and known by its first Hebrew word, *Shema*, the root of the Hebrew word *mashmaut*, which may be translated: "meaning, sense, significance." The origin of the word is the root "to hear."[10] The implication is that meaning must be listened for. *Shema* means "to listen and listen attentively for manifestations of the one and only God, and relate to the *mashmaut*, the meaning, of God's words." Moses couched this concept in the form of a command because he feared that the people, when left to their own resources, would become complacent and forget how to listen for God.

This imperative of attentive listening is reinforced in the musical service of Marc Lavry. His musical notation indicates that the Shema is to be sung pianissimo, as softly as possible, conveying acute awareness to all sensory perceptions which reveal God's presence.

The above translation of the Shema will sound strange to those who grew up reciting "the Lord is One." The variant, "the Lord alone," appears in both the UAHC and JPS Torah commentaries,[m] although *one* is clearly the precise equivalent of the Hebrew *echad*.

The JPS commentary provides the following explanation: "For all its familiarity, the precise meaning of the *Shema* is uncertain, and it permits several

---

[m] UAHC stands for Union of American Hebrew Congregations (Reform). JPS represents Jewish Publication Society (Conservative).

possible renderings. The present translation indicates that the verse is a description of the proper relationship between YHVH and Israel: He alone is Israel's God."[11]

Rabbi Slonimsky held a more expansive view. Rabbi Dannel Schwartz told me how his mentor shocked his rabbinic students by urging, "Ladies and gentlemen, God is not one. God is singular, and man is many. There is no one prevailing or predominate conception of God."

However, the prophecy of Zechariah presents an exception: "On that day the Lord shall be one and His name shall be one" (Zechariah 14:9).

Once again, wisdom from Slonimsky: "*On that day*, not as yet alas, but surely *on that day* He shall be one as He is not yet one. For how can God be called one if humankind is rent asunder in misery and poverty and hate and war? When humankind has achieved its own reality and unity, it will thereby have achieved God's reality and unity. Till then God is merely an idea, an ideal."[12]

Erich Fromm, The Art of Loving, concurred, "He must be made one, and man is the agent in whose hands it is left to make or to mar that supreme integration."[13]

Any confusion about the term *one* will be clarified if we look at the above through our existential prism. In the first sense, Slonimsky refers to the singular God of Israel as having a multitude of perceptions by the many. In the latter sense, God will become "one" when humankind coalesces to authenticate the universality of "Holy you shall be."

This is a concept of monumental importance. It is the over-arching theme of Heschel's seminal opus *God in Search of Man* in which he expressed the thought that God needs man to complete the work of his creation.

What was it Moses wanted Israel to listen for? It was certainly not the elusive concept of the meaning of *one*. He knew better than to leave anything so important to uninformed speculation. Moses ingeniously sought to focus Israel's attention on love of God. At Sinai, he tried to persuade them to love their neighbors and the strangers and to revere God. In Deuteronomy, we find a new dimension of the relationship following on the heels of the *Shema*.

> You shall love the Lord, your God, with all your heart and with all your soul and with all your might. Take to heart these instructions with which I charge you this day. Impress them upon your children. Recite them when you stay at home and when you are away, when you lie down and when you get up. Bind them as a sign on your hand and let them serve as a symbol on your forehead; inscribe them on the doorposts of your house and on your gates.
>
> Deuteronomy 6:5–9

All too often, the idea of love has been so maligned by the rap generation that we must pause to expunge any mundane thoughts from our minds. For insight, we return to Erich Fromm's, *The Art of Loving*: "Love is the active concern for the life and the growth for that which we love. Where this active concern is lacking there is no love."[14]

From the JPS Torah commentary: "Love of God in Deuteronomy is not only an emotional attachment to Him, but something that expresses itself in action. This is in keeping with the fact that Hebrew verbs for feelings sometimes refer as well to the actions that result from them."[15] "You shall love the Lord, your God" is a directive to express that love in benevolent acts.

The Reform Jewish prayer book, *Gates of Prayer*, took cognizance of this by adding a sentence to the above words that follow the Shema, "Be mindful of all My *mitzvoth* and do them; so shall you consecrate yourselves to your God." The path to the love of God is doing his mitzvoth. The Hebrew language is wonderful on this point; it gives us a single word, mitzvoth, meaning both commandments and acts of loving-kindness.

The connection of the doing of mitzvoth with coming to love God is embodied in the first words of the *Holiness Code*: "You shall be Holy, for I, the Lord, am Holy" (Leviticus 19:3). These words of Heschel say it all: "God has instilled in humans something of Himself. Likeness of God is the essence of man."[16]

Humankind can transcend existence and lift itself to a higher level by doing God's will. Virtue is its own reward and the reward of doing a mitzvah is doing another mitzvah. But the ultimate satisfaction of performing good deeds is reflected in love for the One who exemplified love.

Moses' new found eloquence moves to an even higher level in the following:

> See this day I set before you blessing and curse: blessing, if you obey the commandments of the Lord your God which I enjoin upon on you this day; and curse, if you do not obey the commandments of the Lord your God, but turn away from the path which I enjoin upon you this day and follow other gods, whom you have experienced...
>
> When you cross the Jordan to enter and possess the land which the Lord your God is giving to you, and you have taken possession of it and are settled in it, take care to observe all the laws and rules that I have set before you this day.
>
> Deuteronomy 11:26–32

The phrase "I set before you blessing and curse" is one more affirmation of individual free choice in context with an exhortation "to obey the commandments." These words addressed by God to man through Moses are among the most solemn words ever uttered.

> You shall not judge unfairly: you shall show no partiality; you shall take no bribes, for bribes blind the eyes of the discerning and upset the plea of the just. *Justice, justice you shall pursue*, that you may thrive and occupy the land that the Lord your God is giving you. [emphasis mine]
>
> Deuteronomy 16:19–20

Few modern jurists write with such elegance. When my friend and rabbi, Richard Hertz, came to these words, he would look upwards and declaim in stentorian tones, "*Tsedek, Tsedek Tirdof*" ("justice, justice shall you pursue"), as if he were standing in the sandals of Moses facing the Promised Land. It was always a thrilling performance.

"Justice, justice shall you pursue" is the distillation of the Torah's prescription for the civilized ordering of society. No people gave as much loving attention to the overriding importance of law equitably administered and enforced as did Israel. Indeed, Jewish law came to be known as *halacha*, the way to go to fulfill the Divine intent.[17]

We know by now that when a word is repeated a red flag should go up. Repetition in the Torah indicates emphasis, or that several meanings are intended. Had Moses not repeated the word *tsedek*, one might have simply assumed it meant to obey the laws of the land. On the other hand, seeing it twice creates an elegant ambiguity. Was the repetition only for emphasis, or did it call for two or more meanings of *tsedek*?

Clearly, the meaning is in the mind of the beholder, and pondering the question brings forth a rush of ideas. Let me suggest one that has a ring of validity. *Tsedek* has the translation as "justice," but is more frequently rendered as "righteousness," presenting two unique meanings. Thus, we may take the first *tsedek* as the obligation to obey existing laws, and the second to act righteously where there is no law.

Acting righteously without admonition is the pinnacle of ethical behavior. This is congruent with the repetition of *covet* in the tenth commandment.

Moses' knew his last oration would be his final chance to influence Israel. He rose to the challenge by delivering one of the greatest declamations of all time that might be entitled, "The Address for the Welfare of Israel." Rabbi Plaut affirms, "It lays down an enduring foundation for Israel's religion, in that the Torah is declared to be valid for all generations, freely accessible to every member of the people, and not, as among other nations, the possession of a privileged few."[18]

> You have seen all that the Lord did before your very eyes in the Land of Egypt, to Pharaoh and to all his courtiers and to his whole country: the wondrous feats that you saw with your own eyes, those prodigious signs and marvels. Yet to this day the Lord has not given you a mind to understand or eyes to see or ears to hear.
>
> Deuteronomy 29:1–3

This pronouncement is authoritative. Moses did his best to create an awareness of God's labors on Israel's behalf, even though he had difficulty making their stiff-necked progenitors revere Him. It's comparable to driving down a street looking for a building with a specific address. One might have passed by that same building dozens of times and never noticed it before and finally discovering it.

We have eyes to see, but we only see what we are conditioned to perceive. Moses strove to condition the people to perceive what he thought they should see, hear, and understand.

The Israelites witnessed the events in Egypt but were unable to see their implications. As Rabbi Lieberman observed, God was the most tragic character in the Bible. That being the case, Moses ran the deity a close second.

Nehama Leibowitz summed it up beautifully, "God had given them everything—signs, wonders, the parting of the sea, the manna, except the decisive thing—the heart to know."[19]

> As He promised you... I make this covenant, with its sanctions, not with you alone, but both with those who are standing here with us this day before the Lord our God and with those who are not here this day.
>
> Deuteronomy 29:12–14

We've heard this before. It would be easy to understand that Moses recapitulated familiar events because he had a new audience, but why the repetition of ideas before this same audience so uncharacteristic of the Bible? It was due to his increasing frustration.

We need to picture Moses, one of the greatest leaders of humankind, accustomed to being in the forefront of the action, now frustrated by having to lead by persuasion. Moses always thought of himself as the engine, never as the caboose. He anticipated that Joshua, his protégé for forty years, was not sufficiently adept at conditioning perceptions, and he coupled that with Israel's known proclivity to go with the flow. Aware of that, repetition was the only valid alternative.

Moses proceeded to threaten the people, as in Leviticus chapters 24 and 26, with the wrath of God and the detestable things that might befall them, such as exile from the land, if they turned away from the Lord. In despair, he offered this possible sequence of events:

> Perchance there is among you some man or woman, or some tribe or clan, whose heart is even now turning away from the Lord to go and worship the gods of other nations... When such a one hears the words of these sanctions, he may fancy himself immune, thinking, "I shall be safe, though I follow my own willful heart."
>
> The Lord will never forgive him; rather will the Lord's anger and passion rage against that man.
>
> Deuteronomy 29:17–19

The consequences sound horrendous, but there would always be hope of redemption:

> When all these things befall you—the blessing and the curse that I have set before you—and you take them to heart amidst the various nations to which the Lord your God has banished you, and you return to the Lord your God, and you and your children heed His command with all your heart and soul, then the Lord your God will restore your fortunes and take you back in love.
>
> Deuteronomy 30:1–3

Moses' apprehension of freedom of choice is not without reason, nor is it without restitution. The people would always have the choice to amend their errant ways and God would forgive them.

> For the Lord will again delight in your well-being, as He did in that of your fathers, since you will be heeding the Lord your God and keeping His commandments and laws… once you return to the Lord your God with all your heart and soul.
>
> Deuteronomy 30:9–10

In this and intervening verses, the root of the verb *shuv* (return) occurs seven times in various forms. The thrust of the sevenfold *return* is that when an individual turns away, breaches the covenant, God in turn hides his face by turning away. If at a later time sincere repentance is expressed, God returns his face. Heschel's words: "Repentance provides for turning back the clock through a joining of human will and divine acceptance."[20]

Just as the key word of the first ten verses of the chapter was *shuv* (return), we find that the word *chayim* (life) is the motif of the last six verses.

> See, I have set before you this day life and good, or death and evil. For I command you this day to love the Lord, to walk in the ways and to keep the commandments, laws, and teachings of your God, that you may live and increase, and that the Lord your God may bless you in

the land you are about to occupy. But if your heart turns away and you do not listen, but let yourself be lured away to worship other gods and serve them, I warn you now that you will perish, you will not live long in the land which you are crossing the Jordan to enter and occupy,

I call heaven and earth to witness against you this day that I have set before you life or death, blessing or curse; choose life, therefore, that you and your descendants may live—by loving the Lord your God, listening to God's voice, and holding fast to the One who is your life and the length of your days. Then you shall endure in the land which the Lord promised to your fathers, to Abraham, Isaac, and Jacob.

Another match had been struck in the dark as Moses put it all together, and Sartre never said it better.

The choice between life and death was not intended to be taken literally. If one chose to *be lured away to worship other gods*, the choice of redemption would always be an option. Hence, death must be understood as banishment from the social milieu. Certainly, it did not mean literal death from which there could be no redemption.

The alternative was "to love the Lord, to walk in the ways and to keep the commandments... of your God, that you may live and increase." We must then understand life to mean the achievement of one's essence. Heschel taught, "Affinity with God is man's persistent aspiration to go beyond oneself."[21]

The choice was between living and realization of one's authentic self or mere existence and existential failure.

> Moses went and spoke these things to all Israel. He said to them: I am now one hundred and twenty years old. I can no longer be active. Moreover, the Lord had said to me, "You shall not go across yonder Jordan." The Lord your God Himself will cross over at your head; and He will wipe out those nations from your path...
>
> Then Moses called Joshua and said to him in the sight of all Israel: Be strong and resolute, for it is you who shall go with this people into the land the Lord swore to their fathers to give them. And the Lord Himself will go before you.
>
> Deuteronomy 31:1–8

"At the borders of the Promised Land, Moses celebrated the eventual realization of God's will for His people. He sang a hymn of hope to Israel that they will prevail in spirit as well as in body."[22] This became Psalm 90, ascribed to Moses, which begins with the words, "O Lord, You have been our refuge in every generation.

Following the song, Moses blessed the people. He addressed each of the tribes directly and concluded:

> O happy Israel! Who is like you, a people delivered by the Lord, your protecting shield, your sword triumphant! Your enemies shall come cringing before you, and you shall tread on their backs.
>
> Deuteronomy 33:29

Moses went up from the steppes of Moab to Mount Nebo, to the summit of Pisgah, opposite Jericho, and the Lord showed him the whole land... of Judah as far as the Western Sea... And the Lord said to him, "This is the land of which I swore to Abraham, Isaac, and Jacob, 'I will give it to your offspring.' I have let you see it with your own eyes, but you shall not cross there."

So Moses the servant of the Lord died there, in the land of Moab, at the command of the Lord. He buried him in the valley in the land of Moab, near Beth-Peor; and no one knows his burial place to this day.

Deuteronomy 34:1–6

One final verse epitomizes the accomplishments, both historical and theological, of the man who spoke with God.

Never again did there arise in Israel a prophet like Moses—whom the Lord singled out face to face.

Deuteronomy 34:10

THE INNER EAR

S o far, we have avoided the question, "Did Moses as described in the Torah exist?" To those who contend that Moses and the Exodus are fictitious, I would pose this question: "Could a writer not directly challenged by the exigencies of the Grand Narrative have been so creative as to solve the problems, in the way that Moses did?"

Moses' ideas exemplified the highest order of reactionary genius forged in the crucible of adversity. His thinking exemplified by William James' notion "the faculty of perceiving in an unhabitual way" is revealed in his ability to absorb information from his experiences and construct patterns from that information to better understand human behavior, make the people into a cohesive group, and lead them to the Promised Land.

Was his name really Moses? We can't be sure. But that he led whatever number of Israelites from Egypt to the Promised Land and enabled them to feel the presence of the invisible God is without question.

We saw Moses under pressure in Chapter 19, "Scenes Seen Through the Prism," when he spoke to the people after Aaron's two sons had been consumed by fire:

And fire came forth from the Lord and consumed them; Thus they died at the instance of the Lord.

This is what the Lord meant when He said: "Through those near to Me I show Myself Holy, And gain glory before all the people."

Leviticus 10:1–3

Nadab and Abihu had done little, if anything, wrong—certainly nothing to warrant the inhumane, ultimate punishment. Clearly, in reacting to that event, the great mind of Moses was at its spontaneous best. He assuaged the potential anxiety of the people because God had not performed a miracle to spare the lives of the two neophyte priests. He assumed they would recall the apparent omnipotence of God who had provided the plagues, divided the sea, and caused water to flow from a rock.

He further anticipated that the people might reason that God, who had forgiven the calf, would have forgiven most anything—certainly the two young, newly anointed priests who were not experienced in handling fire-pans.

Clearly, this ghastly incident points the way to a different understanding of Moses' conversations with God. He justifiably assumed an editorial privilege by using the alleged words of God as a subterfuge to avoid a breakdown of the concept of a God who could perform miracles but in this case did not. God had failed to come to the rescue of Nadab and Abihu.

The scene brings to mind the symmetry of Genesis and the Grand Narrative. In Genesis, after the duplicitous stealing of the rightful birthright from Esau and its transfer to his younger twin, Jacob, God gradually disappeared from the scene. Later, when Joseph was confronted by the Pharaoh of Egypt, he only referred to what God had said to him.

In the Grand Narrative following Moses' deception after the demise of Nadab and Abihu, his conversations with God became less frequent. Later in Deuteronomy, Moses reported God's intentions without the usual reference to conversations. In both situations, we witnessed the disappearance of God. Symmetry is frequently the source of inferences. It may even lead one to question which event came first, Genesis or the Grand Narrative.

Prior to the conflagration scene, we adhered literally to the Biblical text, only deviating to explain that apparent miracles, such as that the plagues, might be better understood as acts of radical amazement. However, Moses' duplicity following the deaths of Aaron's sons calls into question the numerous conversations Moses had with God. The symmetry of this incident and several that follow prompts us to view preceding incidents in a new light.

The dramatic scene in which God spoke to Moses at the bush, the first of his many conversations, is clouded in the mystery of a typical biblical hiatus. Prior to the event, Moses was doing what he did every day in tending Jethro's sheep. He came to the "mountain of God" where by chance "an angel of the Lord appeared to him in the blazing fire of a bush."

Let us read between the lines and speculate as to what was going on in Moses' mind while tending sheep that day. For years, he had been obsessed with the idea of an invisible God. He yearned fervently to experience His presence, but it had never happened.

A longing for God consumed him. His thoughts became repetitive, like a mantra. His mental focus became more and more narrow and intense. Ultimately, his mind was swept clean of all irrelevances; there was no room in his consciousness for anything but his yearning for God.

In a more lucid moment, he could well have recalled how, as a young man, he had been exposed to the Egyptian belief in mountain deities. Perhaps they were on to something, and he might have thought, *If ever I might find God, it will be on a mountain.*

Exhilarated by the thought of experiencing the presence of the Ineffable Reality, he rushed up the barren mountain, deserting the sheep in his care. There, in his mind's eye, an angel, a manifestation of the Lord, appeared in a burning thorn bush. Because of his feverish anticipation, Moses was unable to look at the flaming bush and turned aside. It was then that he heard God call to him.

This scene and the dialogue with God that followed epitomize the descriptions of mystical experiences as described in Newberg's book, *Why God Won't Go Away*: "The brain's sense of mystical and religious experiences often involve altered perceptions of time and space, self and ego... It is nothing more or less than an uplifting sense of genuine spiritual union with something larger than self."[1]

Brain scans of Tibetan meditators and Franciscan nuns by Dr. Newberg and his scientific team showed that events considered spiritual were, in fact, associated with observable neurological activity. Tibetans and Franciscans obviously have decidedly different spiritual orientations, yet brain studies taken during periods of intense prayer or meditation revealed identical patterns of neural activity in their brains.

Newberg and his associates concluded, "Whatever the ultimate nature of spiritual experience might be—whether it is in fact a perception of an actual spiritual reality, or merely an interpretation of sheer neurological function—all that is meaningful in human spirituality happens in the mind. The mind is mystical by default."[2]

What does this tell us about where the words "*EHEYEH ASHER EHEYEH*" may have come from? My original interpretation about Moses' amazing understanding on first hearing the words was clearly erroneous. The words had already been wired into his mind during his ruminations in the desert. What is even more amazing than my original assumption that he grasped the meaning of the words as the text related is that Moses apparently was having a mystical, existential moment—a recreation of what his mind already knew.

It was through such a process that the words of God got into Moses' head. Newberg explains: "Tracing spiritual experience to neurological behavior does not disprove its realness. If God does exist and if he appeared to you in some incarnation, you would have no way of experiencing His presence except as part of a neurologically generated rendition of reality [auditory, visual, or cognitive]... There's no other way for God to get into your head except through the brain's neural pathways."[3]

Another approach to the question, which reaches substantially the same conclusion, is found in the thinking of Rabbi Abraham Joshua Heschel. In 1959, Temple Beth El, Detroit, sponsored three lectures by eminent Jewish scholars—each challenged to respond to the question, "Who speaks for God?" Unlike those who preceded him, and avoided the issue, Rabbi Heschel was unequivocal in his response. He confronted the question directly, beginning his address by resolutely stating, "This is a fundamental issue; the prophets speak for God."

An enduring memory of the occasion was his aura. He emanated the charisma of one who truly felt the presence of God. It radiated from his demeanor, his physical appearance, and the eloquent phrases he uttered. He urged, "The prophet is overwhelmed by the grandeur of divine presence. In his words the invisible God becomes audible. The thought he has to convey is more than language can contain. Divine power bursts in the words." Heschel also called it divine inspiration, a theme woven throughout the pages of his book *The Prophets*.

In that book, he offered the following passage relating to Moses' awareness: "The consciousness of being approached by God, directly or indirectly, of receiving teaching or guidance, a word or an intimation; the consciousness of living under a God Who calls upon man, turns to him, is in need of him."[4]

These words of Heschel require further explanation. Heschel contended God needed man to get him into the world in order to repair the world; His conduits in search of man were the prophets. As we have seen, Moses felt his mission was to become God's first such emissary.

On that same mountain less than a year after the burning bush, Moses had another undeniable mystical experience as discussed in chapter 15:

> And as Moses came down from the mountain bearing the two tablets of the Pact, Moses was not aware that the skin of his face was radiant, since he had spoken with Him. Aaron and all the Israelites saw that the skin of Moses' face was radiant; and they shrank from coming near him.
>
> Exodus 34:27–31

It behooves us to imagine what occurred between the lines prior to the preceding verses when Moses was alone with God on the mountain. Fortunately, we don't have to imagine, for the eminent Germen novelist Thomas Mann imagined for us:

> What a pressing, oppressive task! He had not measured it beforehand. He had thought only of "writing"—not at all of the fact that one could not just "write." His head glowed and steamed

like a furnace; it was like the top of the peak itself, on fire with the fervor of his hopes for his people. He felt as though rays streamed from his head; as though horns came out of his brow for very strain of desire and pure inspiration.

And he wrote; I mean, he drilled and chiseled and scooped at the splintery stone of the tablets; for these he had prepared beforehand with great pains during the time he spent cogitating his script... Moses rose with the dawn and labored 'till the sun set back in the desert.

We must picture him there, sitting bare to the waist, his breast hairy; coughing now and then from the metallic vapors, and in the sweat of his brow hewing at the tablets, filing and planning. Squatting before them as he leaned against the rocky wall, he toiled away with great attention to detail; first drawing his pot- hooks, his magic runes, with the graver and then drilling them into the stone.[5]

Mann read between the lines with the insight of a novelist to articulately convey the fervid frenzy of Moses when he was so obsessed with devotion to his compelling task. Little wonder "his face was radiant" when he addressed the people—for Moses, a mystical experience was inevitable.

The discernment of the novelist conjoins with the observations of the neurologist to disclose that on both occasions Moses had mystical experiences.

We need to recall a passage in chapter 17, "Moral Grandeur," about Beethoven: "Composed when he was stone deaf and suffering a prolonged and painful dying of cirrhosis, opuses 109–111 reflect Beethoven's soul, his inner being, and the recapitulation of his life—the anguish of his later years amalgamated with the pure joy of music."

For months after writing that paragraph, those three introspective sonatas of Beethoven haunted me. The strains of the slow movements lingered in my mind with thoughts about the peculiar grandeur of his music at its best and the pathos of his deafness. What could be more tragic for a composer than deafness? To one for whom hearing is the essence of his craft, the silent separation from the outside world would have to be devastating. Despite his deafness, this melting beauty of pathetic, introspective wistfulness is seldom found in earlier Beethoven.

Beethoven was able to rise above despair to exultation in these works. The climax of this trio of sonatas features one of the most glorious fugues in all music. It prompted me to listen to Daniel Barenboim's recording of these sonatas repeatedly. Barenboim's poignantly sensitive interpretation coupled with my own ruminations created the feeling of being at one with Beethoven, feeling Beethoven's mystical presence through an auditory experience.

These mystical experiences—my listening to Beethoven and Moses hearing the voice of God when on the mountain—give credibility to two kinds of mystical experience, auditory and cognitive.

We've all had similar experiences that help us understand how Moses, who for months was consumed with the idea of the invisible God, must have felt his presence when alone with his thoughts.

There is no forgetting what happened when I was standing in the hot desert sun in the presence of Jebal Musa. The sight of the mountain alleged to be Sinai triggered a flood of memories associated with Sinai. It all happened in a matter of minutes, so one can only imagine what forty days would do.

The Beethoven experience (music written during the silence of his deafness) led me to thinking about how—despite the absence of auditory stimuli—he heard with his inner ear music more beautiful than any he had conceived prior to his loss of hearing.

There is clearly a Moses/Beethoven pattern emerging from this line of reasoning. What we call hearing can be cognitive and it need not require external stimuli. Is there not an analogy between the experiences of Moses and Beethoven? Moses responded to the deaths of Nadab and Abihu by putting words into the mouth of God: "This is what the Lord meant when He said, 'Through those near to Me I show Myself Holy, And gain glory before all the people.'"

It is apparent that Moses had a mystical experience, which corresponded to Newberg's explanation, "all that is meaningful in human spirituality happens in the mind." Heschel expressed it in nonscientific terms, "The prophet is overwhelmed by the grandeur of divine presence. In his words the invisible God becomes audible."

There is an evident symmetry in the processes by which Beethoven and Moses heard, in one case, grand music, and in the other, the voice of God—both resulted from listening with an inner ear, an inner self, an inner being.

Paraphrasing Dr. Oliver Sacks who expressed a similar thought in his book The Mind's Eye, both men were extremely successful at developing a remarkable power of generating, holding, and manipulating images in their minds.[6] Being of vast sensitivity and overwhelmed by the spirit of their missions, Moses and Beethoven had compelling experiences that were neurologically real.

I cannot depart from the subject without explaining how the experience of hearing Heschel's lecture influenced my thinking. His idea that the prophets spoke for God implies the corollary that God is that which inspired the prophets. These words became a turning point in my search for an understanding of God.

The idea that God can be defined as "that which inspired the prophets" piqued my interest; it remained to discover in what ways the prophets experienced God. What better source than Heschel's book, *The Prophets*, and what better prophet to begin with than Moses, the first and foremost of all; hence, the compelling need to get inside Moses' head to determine how he might have thought.

Surely, when tending Jethro's sheep Moses ruminated on two dramatic incidents in his life, two events of such consequence that the writer included them in the Torah with a hiatus of many years separation. Presumably, he thought that killing the Egyptian guard and protecting

Jethro's three daughters at the well would have been condoned by a humane invisible God as acts of loving kindness. Thinking about them must have given him a warm fuzzy feeling. Years later, he would have identified the feeling as that of divine Presence.

Moses reasoned that God could not be intellectualized; he could only become known through perception conditioned by experience. This was apparent in the name by which he came to know the Invisible, *EHEYEH-ASHER-EHEYEY* (I WILL BE WHAT I WILL BE)—I will be whatever gives humanity a sense of My Presence.

While this realization is a stroke of incredible genius, Moses' process of communicating the concept to the Israelites was equally amazing. One need only consider the ingenuity in creating perceptions of acts of radical amazement in a context so that the Israelites might feel the elusive presence of God. He taught them to grasp through the senses what was hidden from their minds. The culmination of this is expressed in the first commandment, often paraphrased: "I am the Lord your God, who brought you out of the land of Egypt to be your God; I am the Lord your God."

Moses understood that one didn't have to kill a slave or rescue threatened maidens to feel the presence of God. Less dramatic genuine acts of loving kindness would engender a vivid feeling of His Presence. These ideas were delineated in the *Holiness Code*. Here we find the goal of Moses' aspiration to create the proximity of God through Holiness, such acts as loving one's neighbor, ethical living, and observing the Sabbath.

Moses epitomized the wisdom expressed by Heschel: "There is much that philosophy could learn from the Bible. To the philosopher the idea of the good is the most exalted idea. But to the Bible the idea of the good is penultimate; it cannot exist without the Holy. The good is the base, the Holy is the summit. Things created in six days He considered good, the seventh day He made Holy."[7]

Heschel went on to say, "Observance of the seventh day is more than a technique of fulfilling a commandment. The Sabbath is the Presence of God in the world, open to the soul of man. It is possible for the soul to respond in affection, to enter into fellowship with the consecrated day."[8]

The Holiness of the Sabbath is reinforced by one's physical presence in the synagogue. There, one is surrounded by many of the accouterments of the *mishkan* (the tabernacle) with the same intended effects—the eternal light, the menorah, the holy arc, and the reading of Torah. In the synagogue we welcome the Sabbath as a bride and collectively feel God's Presence as we sing and pray together, rejoicing in this special day, which is a gift of his creation.

These emotions call attention to the importance of the *Siddur*, the Jewish prayer-book, which Rabbi Henry Slonimsky regarded as "the most important single Jewish book, a more personal expression, a closer record of Jewish sufferings, Jewish needs, Jewish hopes and aspirations, than the Bible itself. The Jewish soul is mirrored there as nowhere else."[9]

It is somewhat unsettling to discover that subsequent prophets seldom spoke of Moses, but his influence pervaded their lives because all heard with an inner ear. Jeremiah is credited by biblical scholars with setting down the words of Deuteronomy; Isaiah elevated Moses' idea of the Holy to a grand level of exaltation:

Holy, Holy, Holy! The Lord of Hosts!
His Presence fills all the earth.

Isaiah 6:3

And these familiar words of Micah eloquently express the spirit of Holiness:

He has told you, O man what is good,
And what the Lord requires of you;
Only to do justice, To love goodness,
And to walk modestly with your God.

Micah 6:8

Another example of symmetry comes to mind. The subsequent prophets echoed the thoughts of Moses of which these are examples. Heschel summarized the symmetry in resolving the question, "Who speaks for God?" All the prophets spoke for God.

Whereas other scholars, when challenged by the same question, equivocated, Heschel did not. In concluding his address that evening at Temple Beth El, he challenged his audience with the ethical enjoinder, "Emulate the prophets. Make of your lives a work of art."

Why do we emphasize symmetry? It is a useful technique for establishing an abstraction. As used by scientists, for example: the mathematics of string theory is extremely complicated. There are five different concepts of a string, instead of a particle, as being the smallest unit of subatomic matter. Ergo, since all five are symmetrical, symmetry became a nonmathematical validation of string theory.

Many of the ideas we have set forth become more convincing when seen in a symmetrical context. Certainly, the symmetry of Genesis and the Grand Narrative is sufficiently thought provoking to stimulate further academic research.

We now have sufficient information to resolve the question set forth in chapter 6, "Righteous Indignation." Was the trajectory of Moses' mission, his concept of God, engendered by revelation, inspiration, or cognition?

First of all, it's evident that he envisioned the idea of an invisible God to provide moral authority to lead the Israelites from Egyptian bondage and to confront Pharaoh. This act of cognition led to the success of the mission, which transformed the course of human history.

From the time he made the decision until the day of his death, this thought of the invisible God was foremost in his mind. The many imaginary conversations with God, the excursions up and down the mountain, and the ever-present challenges to create perceptions of the Invisible must have engendered many mini-mystical experiences.

Certainly, the continued repetition of such events must have seemed like inspirations from God; Virginia Woolf would have called them, "moments of being."[10] For Moses, repetition would have served to convert cognition to intuition.

These are her words describing "moments of being." She sets forth a fundamental conviction: "From this I reach what I might call a philosophy that behind the cotton wool is hidden a pattern that all human beings are part of a work of art."

Finally, the two monumental mystical experiences atop the mountain must have given him the feeling of a revelation of God's Presence. It follows that Moses might have intuitively thought his response to the pleas of the multitude within sight of the Promised Land came from God as a revelation, even though somewhat disingenuous.

This is not to say that this is how he considered God. It is more like how we might think he felt the Presence of the Invisible. Unfortunately Moses did not have access to our contemporary vocabulary; such expressions as intuition, neural pathways, and existentialism. He was limited by the constraints of whatever ancient mid-eastern languages he spoke.

His sense of reality led him to conclude he was only able to ascend one last mountain, Nebo, for having lost the fire in his bones, he was no longer able to lead Israel into the Promised Land.

As he observed the land of Canaan stretched out before him, Moses could only dream that Israel would "not forget the things they saw with their own eyes…

and make them known to their children and to their children's children." The emphasis was now converted from experiencing to memory. His dream created the evolution of a culture characterized by the indomitable spirit of the Jewish people.

He conceptualized the abstraction that an unseen God could only get into one's head by experiences conditioned to become perceptions—that is, in contemporary parlance, through neural pathways. After the escape from Pharaoh and the pursuing Egyptians, Moses drew on such emotional resources as song, dance, and metaphor to point the way to experience the presence of the Invisible with these inspiring words:

> Who is like You, O Lord, among the celestials;
> Who is like You, majestic in Holiness,
> Awesome in splendor, working wonders!
>
> Exodus 15:11

When he ascended Nebo, never to be seen again, I felt as though I had lost a devoted friend. To convey that feeling there are no more apt words than those Shakespeare expressed through the lips of Juliet at the passing of Romeo:

> "When he shall die,
> Take him and cut him out in little stars,
> And he will make the face of heaven so fine,
> That all the world will be in love with night,
> And pay no worship to the garish sun."[11]

ENDNOTES

The Essence of Torah

1. Daniel C. Matt, *The Essential Kabbalah*, (San Francisco: HarperCollins, 1995), 134.

The Grand Narrative

1. Jan Assman, *Moses, The Egyptian*, (Cambridge, MA: Harvard UP, 1999), 3.
2. From a lecture of Martin Buber, 1926.
3. Israel H. Weisfeld, *This Man Moses*, (Kingsport, TN: Kingsport Press), 137.
4. William James, *Principles of Psychology*, (Canada: Little, Brown, 1992), 546.
5. Talmudic Proverb.

A Match Struck in the Dark

1. Virginia Woolf, *To the Lighthouse*, (New York: Random House, 1991), 183.
2. Rabbi Milton Steinberg, *Basic Judaism*, (Philadelphia: Harvest Book, 1947).
3. Steinberg, 39.

4. Abraham Joshua Heschel, *The Prophets*, (New York: Harper Row, 1978), 222.
5. Rabbi Burton L. Visotzky, *The Road to Redemption*, (New York: Crown, 1998), 15.

Where Is Sinai Today?

1. Martin Buber, *Moses*, (New York: Harper, 1958), 101.
2. David Bakan, *Sigmund Freud and the Jewish Mystical Tradition*, (Boston: Beacon Press, 1975), 127.
3. Jean-Paul Sartre, *The Psychology of Imagination*, (New York: Citadel Press, 1991), 279.
4. Rabbi Irwin Groner, Sermon delivered at Congregation Shaarey Zedek, Southfield, Michigan, January 1986.

Where Sinai Is Today

1. Jean-Paul Sartre, *Essays in Existentialism*, (New York: Citadel, 1993), 31.
2. Sartre, 35.
3. Sartre, 36.
4. Sartre, 34.
5. William Barrett, *Irrational Man*, (Garden City, NY: Anchor Books, 1962), 162.
6. Walter Kaufman, *Existentialism*, (Cleveland, OH: World Publishing, 1956), 12.
7. Plato, *The Republic*, Book VII, (New York: Anchor Books, 1993), 205.
8. Thomas Levenson, *Measure for Measure*, (New York: Anchor Books, 1994), 72.
9. Barrett, 162.
10. Barrett, 115.

11. Shakespeare, *Hamlet*, act I, scene v, line 166.

12. Harold Bloom, *Shakespeare*, (New York: Broadhead, 1998), 281.

13. Shakespeare, *Hamlet*, act III, scene ii, line 25.

14. Levenson, 232.

15. Mark Twain, *A Tramp Abroad*, (London: Chatto & Windus, 1889), 448.

16. Kaufman, 103.

17. Barrett, 188.

18. Will Durant, *Story of Philosophy*, (New York: Simon & Schuster, 1926), 556.

19. Lloyd Morris, *William James*, (New York,: Random House, 1947), 18, 24.

20. Sartre, 31-32.

21. Abraham Kaplan, *New World of Philosophy*, (New York: Random House, 1961), 98.

22. Martin Buber, *Moses*, (London: Horowitz, 1946), 17.

23. Abraham Joshua Heschel, *Moral Grandeur*, (New York: Farrar & Strauss, 1996), 374.

In the Beginning God Was There

1. Richard Elliott Friedman, *The Hidden Face of God*, (New York: HarperCollins, 1995), 30.

2. Burton L. Visotzky, *The Genesis of Ethics*, (New York: Three Rivers Press, 1996), 36.

3. From Heschel's Letter to President Kennedy, June 16, 1963.

4. Friedman, 40.

5. Israel H. Weisfeld, *This Man Moses*, (New York: Bloch, 1966), 139.

The Education of a Prince

1. Martin Buber, *Moses*, (London: Horowitz, 1946), 35.
2. Price, Sellers, and Carlson, *The Monuments and the Old Testament*, 172.
3. Will Durant, *Our Oriental Heritage*, (New York: Simon & Schuster, 1954), 170.
4. Chaim Potok, *Wanderings*, (New York: Knopf, 1978), 65.
5. James Henry Breasted, *A History of Egypt*, (New York: Scribner, 1909), 448.
6. Breasted, 445.
7. Durant, 206.
8. Durant, 206.
9. Bialik & Ravnitzky, *The Book of Legends*, (New York: Schocken, 1992), 61.

Righteous Indignation

1. Bialik & Ravnitzky, *The Book of Legends*, (New York: Schocken, 1992), 64.
2. Chaim Potok, *Wanderings*, (New York: Knopf, 1978), 66.
3. Abbah Hillel Silver, *Moses and the Original Torah*, (New York: Macmillan, 1961), 34.
4. Abraham Joshua Heschel, *The Prophets*, (New York: Harper Row, 1978), 415.

The Grand Encounter

1. Rudolf Otto, *The Idea of the Holy*, Oxford: Oxford Press, 1958), 63.
2. Umberto Cassuto, *Commentary on the Book of Exodus*, (Jerusalem: Magnes, 1951), 37.

3. Samuel Terrien, *The Elusive Presence*, (Eugene, OR: Wipf & Stock, 1978), 119.

4. Walter Kaufman, *Existentialism from Dostoevsky to Sartre*, 142.

5. Nehama Liebowitz, *Studies in Shemot*, (Brooklyn: Chemed Books, 1981), 118.

6. Liebowitz, 53.

7. Sartre, *Nausea*, (New York: New Directions, 1964), 34.

8. Terrien, 116.

9. Ernest Klein, *Etymological Dictionary of the Hebrew Language*, (New York: Macmillan, 1987), 255.

10. Henry George, *Moses—Apostle of Freedom*, address to YMHA, San Francisco.

Show Time

1. Chaim Potok, *Wanderings*, (New York: Knopf, 1978), 67.

2. Nahum Sarna, *Exploring Exodus*, (New York: Schocken, 1986), 70.

3. Gary Greenberg, *Myths of the Bible*, (Naperville, IL: Sourcebooks, 2000), 205.

4. Frerichs & Lesko, *Exodus: The Egyptian Evidence*, (Winoa Lake, IN: Eisenbrauns, 1997), 47.

5. Greenberg, 207.

Radical Amazement

1. Price, Sellers & Carlson, *The Monuments and the Old Testament*, 110.

2. Will Durant, *Our Oriental Heritage*, (New York: Simon & Schuster, 1954), 170.

3. Nahum Sarna, *Exploring Exodus*, (New York: Schocken, 1986), 111.

4. Gary Greenberg, *Myths of the Bible*, (Naperville, IL: Sourcebooks, 2000), 108.

5. Abraham Joshua Heschel, *Moral Grandeur*, (New York: Farrar & Strauss, 1996), 364.

6. Rudolf Otto, *The Idea of the Holy*, Oxford: Oxford Press, 1958), Introduction.

7. Cynthia Ozick, *Metaphor and Memory*, (New York, Random House, 1989), 265.

The Party's Over

1. Mary Ellen Chase, *Life and Language / Old Testament*, (New York: Norton, 1955), 65.

2. Umberto Cassuto, *Commentary on the Book of Exodus*, (Jerusalem: Magnes, 1951), 184.

3. Martin Buber, *Moses*, (London: Horowitz, 1946), 17.

A Matter of Choice

1. Chaim Potok, *Wanderings*, (New York: Knopf, 1978), 71.

2. Nehama Liebowitz, *Studies in Shemot*, (Brooklyn: Chemed Books, 1981), 298.

3. Adapted from Abraham Kaplan, *New World of Philosophy*, (New York: Random House, 1961), 108.

4. William E. Kaufman, *Contemporary Jewish Philosophies*, 82.

5. W. Gunther Plaut, *The Torah Commentaries*, (New York: UAHC Press, 1981), 525.

6. Heschel, *Man Is Not Alone*, 195

7. Rabbi Richard C. Hertz, a sermon delivered at Temple Beth El, Detroit, MI, 1971.

The Ten Utterances

1. *Anchor Bible Dictionary*, Vol. 6, (New York, Doubleday, 1992), 394.
2. Chaim Potok, *Wanderings*, (New York: Knopf, 1978), 72.
3. Burton L. Visotzky, *The Road to Redemption*, (New York: Crown, 1998), 206.
4. Israel H. Weisfeld, *This Man Moses*, (Kingsport, TN: Kingsport Press), 70.
5. Abraham Joshua Heschel, *The Sabbath*, (Canada: Harper Collins, 1951), 75.
6. James L. Kugel, *The Bible As It Was*, (Cambridge, MA: Harvard UP, 1997), 394).
7. *Anchor Bible Dictionary*, 383.
8. Nelson Glueck, *Chesed in the Bible*, (Cincinnati: Hebrew Union College Press, 1967), 88.
9. *The Torah, A Modern Commentary*, (New York: UAHC Press, 1981), 535.

Book of the Covenant

1. Nahum Sarna, *Exploring Exodus*, (New York: Schocken, 1986), 182-189.
2. Cynthia Ozick, *Metaphor and Memory*, (New York, Random House, 1989), 279.
3. *The Torah, A Modern Commentary*, (New York: UAHC Press, 1981), 580.

Alone Atop the Mountain

1. Umberto Cassuto, *Commentary on the Book of Exodus*, (Jerusalem: Magnes, 1951), 319.

2. *The Torah, A Modern Commentary*, (New York: UAHC Press, 1981), 598.
3. Samuel Sandmel, *Alone Atop the Mountain*, (New York: Doubleday, 1973), 167.
4. Frerichs & Lesko, *Exodus: The Egyptian Evidence*, (Winoa Lake, IN: Eisenbrauns, 1997), 111.
5. Harold Bloom, *Jesus and Yahweh*, (New York: Penguin, 2007).

Betrayal

1. Avivah Gottlieb Zornberg, *The Particulars of Rapture*, (New York: Doubleday, 2001), 402.
2. *Anchor Bible Dictionary*, Vol. 6, (New York, Doubleday, 1992), 1068.
3. Talmud Exodus Rabah 43:1
4. Shakespeare, *Hamlet*, act I, scene ii, line 145.

Awe and Transition

1. Jean-Paul Sartre, *Essays in Existentialism*, (New York: Citadel, 1993), 36.
2. Laurence J. Silberstein, *Martin Buber's Social and Religious Thought*, (New York: New York UP, 1936), 161.
3. Silberstein, 127.
4. Umberto Cassuto, *Commentary on the Book of Exodus*, (Jerusalem: Magnes, 1951), 432.
5. Martin Buber, *On the Bible*, (New York: Schocken, 1968), 59.
6. Martin Buber, *On Judaism*, (New York: Schocken, 1968), 151.

7. Avivah Gottlieb Zornberg, *The Particulars of Rapture*, (New York: Doubleday, 2001), 442.

8. James Henry Breasted, *History of Egypt*, (New York: Scribners, 1905), 360-378.

9. Cassuto, 437.

10. Nahum M. Sarna, *The JPS Torah Commentary – Exodus*, (New York: Jewish Publication Society, 1991), 215.

11. Sarna, 216.

12. Martin Buber, *I and Thou*, (New York: Scribners, 1958), 79.

13. Lawrence Kushner, *The Book of Words*, (Woodstock, VT: Jewish Lights, 1995), 27.

14. Newberg, D'Aquili, and Rause, *Why God Won't Go Away*, (New York: Ballantine, 2001), 100.

15. Newberg, D'Aquili, and Rause, 113.

16. Newberg, D'Aquili, and Rause, 146-149.

17. Samuel Sandmel, *Alone Atop the Mountain*, (New York: Doubleday, 1973), 181.

Making the Invisible Visible

1. Rabbi Abraham Ibn Ezra, *The Sabbath Epistle*.

2. Shemoth Rabba 48:7.

3. *Anchor Bible Dictionary*, Vol. 1, (New York, Doubleday, 1992), 899.

4. Jan Assman, *Moses the Egyptian*, (Cambridge, MA: Harvard UP, 1999), 59.

5. Abraham Joshua Heschel, *Moral Grandeur and Spiritual Audacity*, (New York: Farrar & Strauss, 1996), 86.

6. Nahum M. Sarna, *The JPS Torah Commentary – Exodus*, (New York: Jewish Publication Society, 1991), 237.

Moral Grandeur

1. Nehama Leibowitz, *Studies in Vayikra (Leviticus)*, (New York: Chemed Books, 1980), 1.
2. James Henry Breasted, *A History of Egypt*, (New York: Scribner, 1909), 325, 411, 448.
3. Jean-Paul Sartre, *Essays in Existentialism*, (New York: Citadel, 1993), 60.
4. Leibowitz, 22, 33.
5. Leibowitz, 94.
6. Leibowitz, 110.
7. Bernard J. Bamberger, *The Torah: A Modern Commentary*, (New York: UAHC, 1981), 890.
8. Abraham Joshua Heschel, *The Insecurity of Freedom*, (Philadelphia: Jewish Publication Society, 1966), 56.
9. Heschel, *The Insecurity of Freedom*, 165.
10. Erich Fromm, *Man for Himself*, (Greenwich, CN: Fawcett, 1947), 98-107.
11. Jonathan Judaken, *Jean-Paul Sartre and the Jewish Question*, (Lincoln, NE: Nebraska UP, 2006), 236.
12. Abraham Joshua Heschel, *Moral Grandeur and Spiritual Audacity*, (New York: Farrar & Strauss, 1996), 77.
13. Heschel, *Moral Grandeur and Spiritual Audacity*, 79.
14. Bernard J. Bamberger, *The Torah: A Modern Commentary*, (New York: UAHC, 1981), 895.
15. Palestine Talmud, *Nedarim* (9:4).
16. Shabbat 31a.
17. Cynthia Ozick, *Metaphor and Memory*, (New York, Random House, 1989), 278-83.
18. Abraham Joshua Heschel, *The Sabbath*, (New York: Farrar & Strauss, 1951), 104.

19. Everett Fox, *Five Books of Moses*, (New York: Schocken, 1983), 621.
20. Prayerbook, *Gates of Repentance*, (New York: Central Conference of American Rabbis, 1979), 325.
21. Abraham Joshua Heschel, "Grandeur is to fill man with awe." *The Biblical View of Reality*.

The Other Face of God in Leviticus

1. Nelson Gleuck, *Chesed in the Bible*, (Cincinnati: Hebrew Union Press, 1967), 87.
2. Nahum M. Sarna, *The JPS Torah Commentary – Exodus*, (New York: Jewish Publication Society, 1991), 213.
3. Franz Rosenzweig, *Star of Redemption*, (Madison, WI: Wisconsin UP, 2005), 151.
4. Abraham Joshua Heschel, *The Prophets*, (New York: Harper Row, 1978), 383.
5. Peter Shaffer, *Amadeus*, (New York: HarperCollins, 1968), 49.
6. Will Durant, *Our Oriental Heritage*, (New York: Simon & Schuster, 1954), 302.
7. Avivah Gottlieb Zornberg, *The Particulars of Rapture*, (New York: Doubleday, 2001), 272.
8. Heschel, *The Prophets*, 368.
9. Laurence J. Silberstein, *Martin Buber's Social and Religious Thought*, (New York: New York UP, 1936), 161.
10. Russell Edson, "The Floor."

Scenes Seen Through the Prism

1. Chaim Potok, *Wanderings*, (New York: Knopf, 1978), 72.

2. Morris Adler, *The Voice That Speaks*, (New York: UAHC Press, 1981), 1079.

3. Martin Buber, *Moses*, (New York: Harper, 1958), 168.

4. George Santayana, *Reason in Common Sense*, (New York: Dover, 1980).

5. Buber, 184.

6. Everett Fox, *Five Books of Moses*, (New York: Schocken, 1983), 621.

7. Jean-Paul Sartre, *Essays in Existentialism*, (New York: Citadel, 1993), 46.

Choose Life that You May Live

1. Solomon B. Freehof, *Preface to Scriptures*, (Cincinnati: UAHC Press, 1950), 42.

2. Thody and Read, *Introducing Sartre*, (Cambridge: Icon Books, 1998), 43.

3. Jean-Paul Sartre, *Essays in Existentialism*, (New York: Citadel, 1993), 37.

4. Martin Buber, *On the Bible*, (New York: Schocken, 1982), 102.

5. Martin Buber, *I and Thou*, (New York: Scribners, 1958), 79.

6. W. Gunther Plaut, *The Torah, A Modern Commentary*, (New York: UAHC Press, 1981), 1360.

7. Henry Slonimsky, *Essays*, (Chicago: Quadrangle Books, 1967), 62.

8. Plaut, 1361.

9. Plaut, 1371.

10. Karyn Keder, *Dance of the Dolphin*, (Woodstock, VT: Jewish Lights, 2001), 113.

11. Jeffrey H. Tigay, *The JPS Torah Commentary — Deuteronomy*, (New York: Jewish Publication Society, 1996), 76.

12. Slonimsky, 124.

13. Erich Fromm, *The Art of Loving*, (New York: Harper, 1956), 26.

14. Fromm, 26.

15. Tigay, 77.

16. Abraham Joshua Heschel, *The Mystical Element in Judaism*, essay.

17. Plaut, 1461.

18. Plaut, 1535.

19. Nehama Leibowitz, *Studies in Devarim (Deuteronomy)*, (Jerusalem: Eliner, 1962), 293.

20. Plaut, 1544.

21. Abraham Joshua Heschel, *Moral Grandeur and Spiritual Audacity*, (New York: Farrar & Strauss, 1996), xxi.

22. Plaut, 1555.

The Inner Ear

1. Newberg, D'Aquili, and Rause, *Why God Won't Go Away*, (New York: Ballantine, 2001), 29, 101.

2. Newberg, D'Aquili, and Rause, 101.

3. Newberg, D'Aquili, and Rause, 37.

4. Abraham Joshua Heschel, *The Prophets*, (New York: Harper Row, 1978), 440.

5. Thomas Mann, *The Tables of the Law*, (Philadelphia: Paul Dry Books, 2010), 53.

6. Oliver Sacks, *The Mind's Eye*, (New York: Knopf, 2008), 208.

7. Abraham Joshua Heschel, *The Sabbath*, (New York: Farrar & Strauss, 1951), 75.

8. Heschel, *The Sabbath*, 60.

9. Henry Slonimsky, *Essays*, (Chicago: Quadrangle Books, 1967), 120.

10. Virginia Woolf, *Moments of Being*, (Orlando, FL: Harcourt, 1976), 17.

11. Shakespeare, *Romeo and Juliet*, act III, scene ii, line 21.